THE WORKING NOVELIST

By the same Author

★

Novels

MR BELUNCLE

DEAD MAN LEADING

NOTHING LIKE LEATHER

SHIRLEY SANZ

CLARE DRUMMER

Short Stories

THE KEY TO MY HEART

WHEN MY GIRL COMES HOME

COLLECTED STORIES

IT MAY NEVER HAPPEN

YOU MAKE YOUR OWN LIFE

THE SPANISH VIRGIN

Travel

FOREIGN FACES

THE SPANISH TEMPER

MARCHING SPAIN

LONDON PERCEIVED

With photographs by

EVELYN HOFER

(*published in association with William Heinemann Ltd*)

Literary Criticism

BOOKS IN GENERAL

THE LIVING NOVEL

IN MY GOOD BOOKS

The Working Novelist

V. S. PRITCHETT

1965
Chatto & Windus
LONDON

Published by
Chatto and Windus Ltd
42 William IV Street
London W.C.2

*

Clarke, Irwin and Co Ltd
Toronto

Printed in Great Britain by
Butler and Tanner Ltd
Frome and London

To My Wife

The author makes acknowledgment to the editor of
The New Statesman, in which all these essays
originally appeared.

Contents

CONTENTS

FORDIE

"I ONCE told Fordie that if he were placed naked and alone in a room without furniture, I would come back in an hour and find total confusion." Ezra Pound's joke about Ford Madox Ford hits the mark. Confusion was the mainspring of his art as a novelist. He confused to make clear. As an editor, as a source of literary reminiscence, he attracts because he is always sketching his way from inaccuracy to inaccuracy in order to arrive at some personal, translucent truth. His unreliability may have annoyed, but it is inspired.

As a novelist—and he wrote some thirty novels, nearly all forgotten—he is one of those whose main obstacle is his own talent. A Conrad cannot invent; a Lawrence cannot narrate: such deficiencies are fortunate. They force a novelist to compensate, with all his resources, so that we shall hardly be aware of what is lacking and shall, in any case, think it unimportant. Ford is obstructed less by his defects than by the effusiveness of total ability. He has been called brilliant, garrulous and trivial, but what really happened was that, with the exception of *The Good Soldier*, parts of the Tietjens trilogy and most of *The Fifth Queen*, he never sank into the determined stupor out of which greater novelists work. It is comforting to think that the unduly brilliant may eventually have their stroke of luck: *The Good Soldier* is a small masterpiece.

Interest in Ford's work is now reviving in England and in the United States, where technicians are studied with a useful if exhausting piety. Mr Richard Cassell has got in early with a handy, basic investigation, *Ford Madox Ford*. He is alert to the peculiar effects of the Pre-Raphaelites on Ford, the French influence on the English novel of the period, and so on, but does not discuss the curious romanticising of the idea of "the gentleman" which has made Ford seem tiresome and false to the modern reader. The dilemma of "the gentleman" preoccupied Shaw, James, Conrad, Galsworthy, and has even been revived in the latest novels of Evelyn Waugh. It was once a burning topic—one that Forster, with his marvellous aversion to burning topics, ignored. But there are overtones in Ford's writing on the subject which recall his own criticism of what the Pre-Raphaelites felt about love—they swooned. Swooning about love was a way of not knowing the facts. Ford swooned about the country gentry, and nothing dates so much as fashion in love.

Still, *The Good Soldier* survives the swooning over the character of Colonel Ashburnham and does so because, for once, Ford had his excessive gifts under control. For once he remembered that if he was to be an Impressionist writer, he had better not confuse writing with painting. The confusion of memory need not be coloured; indeed, in writing, if the parts are too prismatically brilliant, the whole will become grey instead of luminous. As this novel shows, Ford was equipped by intelligence and by grief to be a moralist once he could be freed from the paint-box and, above all, from High Art. Conrad must have been a very bad influence on a man who had already too much vagueness in him; Henry James can have only been harmful to one with already so much consciousness. To them Art did nothing but good; the idea is excellent in itself; but it is dangerous to a man of talent who only very seldom in a laborious literary life hits upon a subject that draws out all his experience.

The Good Soldier and *The Fifth Queen* succeed. The former has the compact and singeing quality of a French novel; it is a ruthless and yet compassionate study in the wretchedness of conventional assumptions and society's war upon the heart. The latter is a historical romance and tells the story of Henry VIII and Katharine Howard; it suffers a little from Ford's chronic allusiveness, but a great issue is at stake and the ambiguities in it awaken all his interest in intrigue. His mind was one that hated conclusions, not because it was a sceptical mind but because it wanted to be put to one more test. From this spring his ingenuity as a story-teller—a gift so rare that it is often scorned—and his constant concern with technique. Critics have usually praised this technical capacity, but have said that this was all he had; yet it is—and one ought not to have to say so—a capacity of enormous importance. (Imagine that Jane Austen had left *Sense and Sensibility* in its epistolatory draft!) One can see that to a mind as given to confusion and to posture as Ford's was, technical capacity was his one reality. He asks nothing better than to be seen making difficulties work for him. The famous device of the "time-shift", which was a mania with him, enabled him to begin his scene in the middle and yet arrive with a whole tale of suspense that was thick with suggestion and memories caught on the way ashore.

In *The Good Soldier* the time-shift enabled him to effect those dramatic revaluations of people which give his novels their point. We had supposed, for example, that Leonora was vulgarly jealous when she slapped Mrs Maidan's face; but in a page or two we dart back in time to discover that there was another and stronger motive, one that exposes a hidden part of Leonora's nature: her shocked frigidity, her greed for money. When that is threatened, her passion for appearances collapses. In choosing for the narrator a dull and unemotional man who fumbles his way through a tale of passion which leads to death and madness, Ford has found someone who will perfectly put together the case of the heart versus conventional society, for he is a mild American Quaker perpetually astonished by Catholic puritanism. Meanwhile his own do-gooding wife is, unknown to him, a destroyer and nymphomaniac. Ford is often accused, by the hospital nurses of criticism, of triviality, but in this book the trivia are sharp and enhance the awful dull force of the tragedy.

Re-write *The Good Soldier* in straightforward narrative and Ford's vision of life as a minutely operating process of corrosion vanishes, and with that, of course, his particular Catholic outlook. Corrosion, as it is presented in this novel, means that we have more parts to our lives than one and that they work fatally upon each other. One has a quite extraordinary sense in the book of the minds of people perpetually thinking away their heartbeats.

Ford's preoccupation with technique—point of view, time-shift, *progression d'effet*, rendering and so on—was both a godsend and a curse, for he was constitutionally distracted, impatient and shy of coming to terms. By concentrating on the *means* of creating an impression he seems to have hoped, in some of his novels, to find that the means would suggest an End darker, more inscrutable and mysterious, than anything in the author's mind at the outset. Life was an intrigue that was never resolved, a meaningless experiment. This approach might lead, as it does in the works of Conrad, to fogginess; in Ford it could lead only to an excessive high-lighting of detail and to staginess. The secret, Romantic Ford leans too much on the ominous and sardonic outsider, the shadow figure breathing heavily down the neck of the reader, Art pretending to be Destiny. But when Ford is at one with his subject, as he is in *The Fifth Queen*, he stages well. His delight in playing fast and loose with time, in beginning a scene in the middle of a broken sentence, dropping it and picking it up again until the crisis is built up, his whole patterning and puzzling, are vividly justified.

He succeeds, more often than not, in his ingenious system

of getting at the inside of things by looking intensely at the surface alone. This, of course, he inherited from the painters. He may see more than we can in the way people's hands lie in their laps, or how their legs look when they are kneeling, or how much of Henry VIII appeared as he went upstairs; but in the larger pictorial actions—Tom Culpepper rushing up drunk from Greenwich to Smithfield eager to see some martyrs at the stake because he'd never seen a burning before —the sense of daily life dancing by in a man's mind is wonderfully conveyed. Ford was a master of episode. If he is stagey, he does not ham. We notice, for example, that Tom Culpepper doesn't in fact see the actual burning because he gets into an absurd brawl. As a story-teller Ford recognised life when he saw complication and chance. His brutal scenes are benevolently comic; his women are originals; wherever there's human naivety and deviousness he is as happy as Kipling was, but with compassion. And throughout there is no detail that fails to bear on the religious quarrel which is his central subject. He responded very much in all his work to the margin men and women leave in their minds, to their long-headedness; and one can see that he found a parallel between the corruption of the Reformation and that of the Edwardian world which had killed the heart, he would have said, by reducing virtue and honour to the condition of masks.

No doubt *The Fifth Queen* is too close to the eye in a cinematic way to have the spacious historical sense of a great historical novel like *Old Mortality*; it hasn't the coolness of Mérimée's superb short novel, the *Chronicle of Charles* IX; but it makes most of our historical fiction up to 1914 look like the work of interior decorators. Literature for Ford was a passion; its rituals were sacred. But there is no doubt about his moral seriousness or the cumulative effect of the main story. How, by what stages, will Katharine bring the

King to the point of making his submission to Rome? How will the King procrastinate? What lies will trap the Queen? Will the King, for once, be able to escape from his changeable and fatally political nature? What belongs to Caesar, what to God—and what to Good Learning? There is nothing allusive in the handling of this massive central conflict and it is brought to its climax without melodrama. One thing Impressionism could do was to catch the day as it passed through the minds of the actors in it. It could record confusion by a scrupulous and ingenious use of the means of art. Allowing for Ford's pleasant vanity in the imposture, this bravura piece—as Graham Greene calls it in his introduction to the Bodley Head collection of Ford's stories—is rather fine.

Half-English, half-German and, by fancy, French, Ford Madox Ford was nature's expatriate. His only country, he said, was literature. To be precise, it was "the Novel". He simply lived for it. Consider him as an incurable and dedicated work of fiction, one of the most diverting yet serious and instructive of "living lies", and he becomes comprehensible. As a brilliant human being he was self-dispersing, moving from one hallucination to another, dumping his luggage in the hotel room of two or three cultures; he reassembled himself, for a while, in words and stories and in them he believed with an industrious and short-lived intensity. He succeeded in only three remarkable stories—*The Good Soldier*, the *Fifth Queen* trilogy and *Parade's End*. They vindicate his happy yet tortured incapacity to go straight from a starting-point, for he had none. They put his lack of self-confidence, his shortness of spiritual breath, his indolence, to use. They brought out and exploited with full resource the price he had to pay for his extraordinary cleverness: the emotion of anguish. One is tempted to say "passion" also—but one has to hesitate here. The writers who convey passion also convey the terrible calm of its purgation and aftermath and Ford is too full of his own skill and ironical humour to allow that. But he does leave us with an indignant sense of unforgettable pain. One always finds that at the bottom of the baggage Ford left about the world.

Some pain is self-sought—the pain, for example, of our choice of impossible incarnations. It is hard, here, to separate the factitious from the inevitable. When he became incarnate as Tietjens in *Parade's End*, Ford could not obliterate Ford. One does not want him to do so, for Tietjens is Ford's anguished hallucination. No novelist can completely become another character; in Tietjens Ford constructed an English gentleman as only something like German romanticism or idealism could see him. Ford was no gentleman; he was a fine artist. He seems minutely to have observed the type, and at the same time to have loaded him with history and an inhuman willingness to suffer everything for the sake of suffering. So often one has seen expatriates find their home in a past that has not existed: Ford's plain feudal Yorkshire squire, with his love of the pre-industrial way of life, his scorn of the vulgar modern world, his dislike of ambition, his irritable abstention, his martyred sense of decency, looks today like a romancing not about a man but a code.

When Ford created Tietjens the dilemma of the gentleman was very much the fashion, as I have said. These talented agrarians existed. The coarse businessmen, speculators and careerists were breaking in on them, the press had turned yellow, the conventions were shocking when they worked and even more shocking when they did not. If Tietjens and his scruples about sex and society seem odd now, they did not fifty years ago. Rock-like before the unanswered slanders of his bankers, his military friends, his father, his cold, promiscuous wife who tricked him over the paternity of his child, Tietjens was exactly the figure to expose by his silence and his suffering the rottenness of Edwardian society. Further, he was not a Roman Catholic but his wife was, and the curse on the Tietjens family is thought to go back to the Reformation and the thieving of Roman Catholic lands. This adds to Tietjens's martyrdom, a touch of destiny which is pretty gamey stuff. That old row has been hung too long to be digestible. One is rather exasperated by Tietjens's stubborn determination to collect all the slings and arrows going; after all, where does the family get its millions from? From the sacred soil of a great estate? Hardly. Towards the end of the novel there is a hint that the family controls a lot of industry in Middlesbrough. Tietjens is just as much a child of the industrial revolution as anybody else. He may not like the men of the new order who were coming in just before 1914: not being gentlemen they were certain to cheat. But isn't he simply an idealiser of convention? One has a sneaking sympathy for his wife, who at one moment complains that her husband is trying to be Jesus Christ as well as the misunderstood son of a great landowner. Her cruelties are an attempt to turn a martyr into a man.

In creating Tietjens, Ford chose a character utterly unlike himself and did the detail admirably. He caught the obtuse pride of the social masochist. He caught the spleen of the gentleman because this accorded well with the ironic spleen that Ford himself felt as an artist, even when it was a pose. The gregarious, voluble, intelligent nature of Ford could not be prevented from mingling with the Yorkshire squire; what one does not accept in Tietjens is the romantic German aura. Any German can do a better job of being an English gentleman and Tietjens is just a Germanised squire. He is even a classical scholar.

Two more able American critics, John Meixner* and Paul Wiley†, have written studies that will stimulate the

* *Ford Madox Ford's Novels*, University of Minnesota Press, 1963.
† *Novelist of Three Worlds*, Syracuse University Press, 1962.

Ford addict, and both agree that *Some Do Not* is the best of the Tietjens novels. It is a complete "Affair"; the famous time-shifts are well-patterned. And both understand that Ford, being an indolent man with little self-confidence and an observer before everything else, was best at beginnings. Any paragraph is better than a page. All the good things, large or small, are beginnings. The boredom we experience in Ford comes, indeed, from the strain of reading innumerable beginnings on every page. So these critics find that Tietjens does not grow. His wife turns melodramatically wicked as the book goes on. I don't entirely agree with the first part of the verdict: Tietjens may be better done in the earliest volume but he becomes more representative and important as a human being in the account of the war in France, and especially because his puzzling private life is in abeyance.

Ford's response to the war brought out his highest quality: his historical sense and his exactitude. He surveyed with sardonic relish the chaos of the staff officer's labours: the numbering and allotting, the terrible paper-work in a war no one understood. The Canadians are going up the line, but where are they? They have been held up somewhere by a train smash. What is to happen to the men they are supposed to relieve? Ah, now the Canadians have been found! And now we've got them, the orders have been countermanded. The intrigue and the rot at the Base produce a natural defensive reaction: the chaos is intended by the politicians, the *embusqués* at home. And who are they? The new men, of course, the climbers and careerists. (This certainly was the legend of the period.)

The general picture of a whole society floundering is done with a wonderful precision and not in the form of easy diatribe. Tietjens is just the right kind of numbed Homeric figure to record the sudden killing of a man in the staff dug-out, a man to whom he had refused leave; or the explosion of a mine and the rescuing of the buried. As a character Tietjens escapes from the cliché of almost all the war novels of that time in which the hero conveys that the whole war has been declared against him personally. Tietjens knows that a civilisation, or at any rate a class, is sinking. Responsible and capable, Ford-Tietjens has an unselfed and almost classical sub-Olympian view of the experience. Although he was self-consciously an impressionist, Ford has some inner sense of a moral order. Or, if not that, a moral indignation at the lack of it. Or, if not that, a taste for the moral consolations of defeat. He brings not only an eye but a judgment to what he sees.

There is something odd but also—from a novelist's point of view—tolerant about this judgment. A craftsman, through and through, in everything, Ford is interested in the way things are done. Even corruption has its curious status. What are gunners like, what are their interests, their follies, what is the *virtu* of the trade? He is deeply interested in the idle detail of human nature and his own lazy aloofness enabled him to catch the detail perfectly. A variety of scenes comes to mind: the death of O Nine Morgan or the astonishing scene where a gunner chases a solitary German with shells.

> His antics had afforded these gunners infinite amusement. It afforded them almost more when all the German artillery on that front, imagining that God knew what was the matter, had awakened and plastered heaven and earth and everything between them for a quarter of an hour with every imaginable kind of missile. And had then abruptly shut up.

And it had all happened merely because Tietjens had lightly told a gunner that any Italian peasant with a steam-plough could pulverise a field at a cost of thirty shillings, which was cheaper than the cost of high explosives. As a craftsman the gunner was put on his mettle.

That incident is anecdotal, but Ford could create the

people who lived the anecdotes. His art—particularly the theory of the time-shift—was in part based on an analysis of talk, the way it plunges and works back and forth. The method was perfected in *The Good Soldier*; in the later, Tietjens novel, it does not succeed so well. It often becomes a device for refusing to face a major scene. One has only a confused notion of what went on in the hotel bedroom when the drunken General broke in on Tietjens and his wife at a crucial point in their sado-masochistic relationship, when it is important that we should know all. Ford's view seems to have been that no one ever quite knows what goes on at the crucial moments of life. His craftsmanship becomes obscurely crafty at such moments, as though, with tiresome cleverness, he had decided that it was the business of art to impose chaos on order. At his worst, he turns never saying Yes and never saying No into an aesthetic neurosis.

Where do we place Ford in relation to the contemporaries he admired—James and Conrad? For Mr Meixner Ford was "locked in the prison of his own theories" and lacked "the personal audacity, the conquering boldness", required by a masterpiece. He was a penetrating historian, a man of fundamental insights, but he did little with them; his ingenuity made him intellectually thin. *The Good Soldier* succeeds because it is done in the first person, which allows him to rid himself of the stiff aloofness and impersonality he thought he was copying from the French—by a paradox this is his unmistakably French novel. He has not the range of a James or a Conrad, nor the mass of good work; but Conrad's characters are "static and inert", despite the subtlety and penetration of his analysis; and Ford (for Mr Meixner) surpasses Conrad in *The Good Soldier* and *Some Do Not* because Ford's people have great inner life, are more various, more real, more fluid and more pleasing and more moving. I would have thought Conrad's sceptical moral sense, as a *déplacé*, was richer than

Ford's. Compared with James, Ford goes deeper (for Mr Meixner) into the range of spiritual terror and anguish. If, after a lot of wrangling, one came to agree with this last point, one would have to qualify it by saying that the very nature of Ford's methods made these depths brief and rare; and that they came as a result of calculated shock. We feel the shock felt by Tietjens when O Nine Morgan is killed before his eyes; we are startled by the picture of Tietjens trying to recover his memory when his brain has been affected by bombardment—but these episodes remain superb fragments.

Mr Wiley is good at showing the consistency of Ford's career as a novelist and as theorist of the novel and pays a lot of attention to the forgotten works. Although the discussion of Ford's methods, in his last novel, *Vive le roy*, is interesting, it does not succeed in making this maddening work more readable. Like a first-class teacher Ford gives his ideas the force of his personal life. But, except in his two best books, he had so many ideas that he was exhausted by the time he got to the page. He had not the breath. He creates the spell of someone always on the move; the pen itself was expatriate. His theories, in the end, become devices for postponing the novelist's task: which is to settle and confront. Impressionism —and with it a desire to impress—becomes an unconscious journalism. One sees him, and his characters also, wearing themselves out by continually changing trains.

THE FORSYTES

GALSWORTHY? A City toff, decent fellow, fond of the Turf. Good shot. A bit damp-eyed. Some trouble with a woman. Gave up shooting birds, took to novel-writing and shooting his own class—rich lawyers, company directors—until the Germans unsportingly cleared the covers. In the end, wrote telegraphese like this and forgave all. "The rum thing to me," said Gilbert Murray who admired *The Forsyte Saga*, "is that I don't feel that I know in the least what a Forsyte is like and I am not conscious of having seen one." This is not Oxford snobbery: after forty-odd years one feels exactly that. Galsworthy's imagination was lukewarm: thin, partial, thumb-nail sketches of people, poor invention, jog-trot realism, blur when there is a question of feeling, embarrassment or jauntiness when there should be thought.

On the other hand, D. H. Lawrence *did* jump at Forsyteism as a social illness and even respected the satirical force of *A Man of Property*. It opens well and has an idea. Before the family history drifted into genteel soap opera, thousands of readers recognised their relatives; on the Continent and in America, the *Saga* became the standard guide to the English character. Even today, especially on the other side of the Iron Curtain, "the great Galsworthy" is brought out like a trump card when one is playing a hand or two with foreign intellectuals. The world has a hunger for the single, simple explanation and Galsworthy explained where the Victorians had put on a complex, congested, preaching face.

For him property was the English passion; convention disposed of the inconvenient emotions. You bought everything

—from houses, pretty country, works of art, to women and children. Every human feeling had to pass through a more or less brutalising shareholders' meeting; it had somehow to pay and, if you had your losses, you put a soothing cream of sentiment over them. The foreigner brought up on Victorian impenetrability was ready for Galsworthy's inside view. It explained that peculiar foreign fantasy: the well-off, buttoned up, blue-eyed, blank-faced Englishman who was a sort of gun dog to a master called the Right Thing and trained to love life only when it was decently dead. In short, the Forsytes are "rum" because they are a theory. The theory works in *The Man of Property* because Galsworthy's anger is roused; once that dies, the *Saga* becomes a family charade and a hymn to crustiness.

A man of property himself, Galsworthy was a rebel against his own class for reasons of chivalry rather than of deep principle. His private story is very relevant—too relevant. It has long been known and Mr Dudley Barker has written a mild, tactful and, occasionally, sceptical account of it in a biographical study, *The Man of Principle*. A young man with a handsome allowance and pleasant expectations, Galsworthy amused himself with horse-racing and not much more at Oxford; came down to idle at the Law; was sent round the world to get over a mild, unsuitable love affair; returned to discover religious doubt, guilt about the condition of the poor, and to slip into a liaison with his cousin's wife. In the mercantile euphemism for describing sexual unhappiness, the couple were not "on terms": even worse, she played Chopin and he preferred the Yeomanry. The fear of scandal, the certainty of ostracism and the danger of hurting his father and, possibly, losing his income kept the liaison fairly secret for ten years. Then the affair blew up. The central theme of *A Man of Property*—the indecency of property rights in love—was provided. Try to own Beauty and it vanishes.

But once the scandal died down and the divorce was over and the ostracism of Ada Galsworthy came to an end, Galsworthy's rebellion ended too. He continued all his life to be indignant about cruelty and social injustice, but within the system. He became a very likeable kind of English crank and this crankiness found an effective outlet in his plays; but as a novelist he sank back into an ironical apologia for the class he represented. Soames, the villain, the only character of any account in *The Forsyte Saga*, becomes Soames the stoic, bearing the weight of his own dull, tragic compulsion to possessive love. That development is commendable. Galsworthy has at least seen that possessive men who put a money value to everything are not thereby cut off from tragic or, at any rate, pathetic experience: if Soames is mean, he is also emotional and, in stoicism, he gains a pitiable strength. But gradually Soames becomes Galsworthy's mouthpiece and that is a betrayal of the meaning of the first volume of the *Saga*. Galsworthy has not the talent, the vitality, the conviction to deepen an idea.

One realises that Galsworthy is not going to face everything out when one sees his handling of the Soames-Irene-Bosinney situation. All that is said conveys nothing about Irene and everything of the Narcissism of those who admire her: they are caressing their own feelings. She is a sentimental mystery —an erotic dream. If she were not, Galsworthy would have to come out with the plain fact that she is a real female, as ruthless as Soames and indeed a bitch in all the crises of the story. Defending his study of erotic passion in an earlier book, *The Dark Flower*, Galsworthy said too much had been written about the physical realities of erotic passion, too little of its spirit; the truth is that he goes straight into sentimentality by a high-minded evasion of the facts. The famous passivity of Irene is a fantasy: she must be seen as the victim. We must be prevented from seeing that Beauty is making victims of her two husbands and her son. For there is a Galsworthian theory that irresistible Passion comes uncalled for in our lives, transfiguring, destroying, vanishing. So it may, but at least we know what and who hits us. The novelist who does not know will be guilty of one of those moral tergiversations that are fatal to his quality as a writer and even to his craftsmanship. Galsworthy is so bemused by Irene that he cannot even get the woman to speak except in lines that sound like bits of a breathless telegram. And she is, more often than not, sitting by an open window near flowers! Clever woman!

After this central failure, Galsworthy is left to exercise the skill of a gentleman amateur on the surface of social life. Here and there he practises a port-wine irony in his little sketches of testy old men and foolish aunts. There are embarrassing pictures of un-Forsyte-like artists. There are one or two good boardroom scenes, for Galsworthy had observed company meetings when he was idling at the Law. There is some expert comedy: Soames, in Paris, mistaken by a detective for his wife's lover. Or the break-up of horse-racing Montague Dartie's rickety marriage, where the manœuvres intended to separate the couple only succeed in re-uniting them. Galsworthy's lapses into the raffish are good.

The interesting thing about him is that he was a taught writer: his wife above all, then Edward Garnett, Conrad, a whole committee, worked on his manuscripts in a manner that would have been intolerable to a less determinedly masochistic figure. He slaved away, like a Forsyte at the office, until he attained a non-stop facility which was his personal triumph and, in the end, his downfall. What no one detected was that his weaknesses fitted him for the stage: his simple sentimental view of the class situation, his feeling for moral melodrama, his eye for the short scene, his topical sense of justice and a reformist temper made acceptable by dialogue done in off-hand remarks. He could knock off a play in a few weeks without help from the committee; and actors gave life to what, in his novels, was really lifeless.

It is fashionable to think him crude as a dramatist; and his situations are really head-on collisions in unlikely circumstances. But he got the admiration of Shaw, and even Wells, who was no admirer of the novels, was won over. The fact is that Galsworthy was an ingenious craftsman. The sudden entrance of the exquisitely serpentine Jew in gorgeous dressing-gown, among a group of the squirarchy struggling into their boiled shirts in the country-house scene of *Loyalties*, "tells" symbolically and theatrically in an instant. Galsworthy also hit the taste of a decade in which—as Mr Barker says—the Welfare State began to kick in the womb. Plays like *The Silver Spoon*, *Strife* or *The Skin Game* had much the same effect on its first audiences as *Look Back in Anger* has had in our own time. He had hit upon that mysterious thing—the idiom of a period. The theatre was just the place for those black-and-white notions of Decency and Vice, Property and Poverty, Truth and Pharisaism which were buried in the confusions of his mind. His novels, he once said, were not social criticism, they were "spiritual examinations", conversations between two halves of himself.

As a man Galsworthy was the gentlest of toffs, and a moral toff to the end. Guilty about his inherited wealth, he scrupulously gave away large sums of money to the needy, to hangers-on, to causes and still managed to leave £98,000. He was a soft touch for ex-convicts. He was whimsical about the enormous list of good causes he supported. They ranged from prison and divorce reform, the establishment of a minimum wage in sweated industries, woman's suffrage, slum clearance, down to the protection of prostitutes and animals and the improvement of slaughter-houses. His generosity to servants and tenants infuriated his neighbours. Yet he remained very much "the man at the club window"—a phrase of Edward

Garnett's that rankled—in the sense that he found it hard to make real contact with people outside his own class. As Mr Barker says, he had no notion that the poor had their own life. He was always the district visitor, solemn, formal and modest.

Galsworthy's character appears most clearly in his relations with Ada Galsworthy. She was the daughter of an eccentric doctor who spent many years building an elaborate mausoleum for himself and used to sit in Norwich cemetery gazing at it with pleasure and thinking of little touches to add to it: an apt progenitor for the original of the mysterious, passive, silent Irene. As a muse—a model from whom the novelist was rarely separated—she was, not surprisingly, exigent. She became a hypochondriac and he was her continual nurse. He said that he had found a talent for nursing. In a sense, he wanted to nurse England. He also said, with a sort of helpless pleasure, that Ada paralysed him. That is a Forsyte story that was never written.

THE KNIGHTSBRIDGE KENNELS

WHY do the novels of Ada Leverson survive? How is it that these water ices of the Edwardian drawing-room have kept their crispness and have not melted away? One can put it down to the Wilde revival; one can regard it as a side effect of the present turdish taste for chichi; or as a passing nostalgia for the tritenesses of a small, safe, set, satiny world of tea-cups and little dinners, where the gravest dangers are things like being seen riding in a hansom with a wan Bohemian girl from the wrong side of the Park. Ada Leverson's urban males are vulnerable to pity for ill-provided females through whose designs any well-appointed woman can see. We are offered a life lived according to "the rules", which smoothly prevent the emotions from becoming more than inconvenient. To cover the inevitable boredom there are always the bitchings and counter-bitchings of the Knightsbridge kennels. Thus, a rather too jolly Mr Mitchell will be "almost any age between 60 and 65"; a Sir Charles is "distinguished to the very verge of absurdity". All this is pleasant enough, but —I agree with Colin MacInnes who writes an ardent preface to Ada Leverson's best-known trilogy *The Little Ottleys*—it has little to do with her merits. The only unconvincing touches that occur in her last novel are those that are closest to the modern world: they record one or two glimpses of the outbreak of the 1914 war. It is natural that they should be unconvincing, for that war killed the comedy of manners. She survives because she is an original and considerable artist.

A writer can be a considerable artist without being more than a minor novelist. If they are to last, the minor novelists depend on sparkle, a freshness of view and a perfection of means; if they are comedians, on the gift of living in a perennial present. Economy and distinction of style and—in Miss Leverson's case—skill in construction are indispensable. They must delight in their limits if we are to delight in them: they must always refuse—and how few middling novelists do make this refusal!—to borrow the courage of other people's convictions. Miss Leverson understood this. It is possible that the pleasure she gives owes a lot to a clever adaptation of the methods of the theatre: the two-dimensional tale passes as quickly as an expert charade. A scene never lasts too long; it is as sharp as repartee. She is careful, even when moralising, to keep to the surface of life and it is often when she appears to be most trivial that she is life-enhancing and most serious.

To the somewhat extravagant praise given by Mr MacInnes, I would add the warning that she has not the range of, say, an Edith Wharton; and although it is true that, in a general way, she writes in the tradition of Congreve, she dilutes with the very different comedy of *The Diary of a Nobody*, the Ottleys being the Pooters, but younger and smarter and moved from Finchley to Knightsbridge. They are little Somebodies. This is the comedy of "life's little ironies" which came in during her lifetime. When the clownish Bruce Ottley and his wife chase from one Hamilton Place to another in London looking for where they are supposed to be dining and find they have got the week wrong; above all, in Bruce Ottley's querulous time as an amateur actor, we have pure Grossmith:

"I told Mitchell what I thought of him in very plain terms. I went so far as to threaten to throw up my part, and he said, 'Well, all right, if you don't like it you can give it up any time.' I said 'Who else could you get at the last minute to play a footman's part?' and he said 'Our footman.' "

The other strain in her comedy is her concern for integrity. She rejoices in the banality of her characters; but in her heroine, Edith Ottley, she has created a young wife who clings to the conservative conventions of her world yet is disturbed to find that she may in her marriage be sacrificing herself to them when she supposes she is doing something sensitive and fine. In other words, Miss Leverson introduces the question of personal truth into her comedy. There is a point at which Edith, despite her coquettishness, is in danger of becoming as tiresome as Thackeray's Amelia; it is no great credit to Edith's probity that she is rescued from having to solve her dilemma by her husband's inane flight with the chief comic character of the book and, ultimately, by the breakdown of the standards of Knightsbridge in the war. I find Edith a shade calculating. Her asinine husband is at his shamefaced worst when the marriage collapses and, in a wonderful scene, comes out with the one honest remark of his life, a ridiculous, fierce *cri de cœur* that punctures the basic assumption of her ethic and her comedy:

"No, Edith. I can't endure married life any longer. It doesn't suit me."

This cry from a prime domestic fusspot who is always carrying on about being master in his own house is marvellously funny, but it has a wildness about it suggesting that the Ottleys, like the rest of this Edwardian world, had somehow begotten two children without having done more than meet socially.

It is sometimes said that artificial comedy in English suffers from a lack of brain. It really celebrates the English genius for hardening off, refusing to face issues and creating an ennui which will be the great guarantor of social, moral and emotional eventlessness. The most boring and self-centred of men, Bruce Ottley, thrives on bordeom and develops, in consequence, a character so eccentric that it never ceases to fascinate his friends. Our comedy, like our way of life, depends on the evasion of ideas or knowledge and on the creation of character. Edith is about to marry a fine fellow at the end of the novel, but as far as comedy is concerned he is a dead loss: he bores us with his £5,000 a year and his undoubted enlightenment. And it is an odd conjunction of life and art that, after she wrote this novel in 1916, Miss Leverson wrote no more.

But she had by then created a comic character far more original than the lunatic Bruce—Madame Frabelle. This portrait is satisfying because it is not caricature. It is the truth about Madame Frabelle that is so funny; and the fact that she is a likeable monster makes her funnier. She is the Life Force gone dowdy, shady and kind, but never dormant. Indeed, advancing years make her phoneyness redoubtable. It is she who runs off with Bruce in the end—one can imagine her picking him up like a puppy in her teeth and wobbling off with him—and anyone who is interested in skill in writing must admire the cleverness with which Miss Leverson insinuates the stages that lead to this dénouement. The splendid thing about Madame Frabelle is that she is absurd, false, but sympathetic—this comes from Miss Leverson's truthfulness:

> Madame Frabelle (of course) was dressed in black, *décolletée* and with a good deal of jet. A black aigrette, like a lightning conductor, stood up defiantly in her hair. Though it did not harmonise well with the somewhat square and *bourgeoise* shape of her head and face, and appeared to have dropped on her by accident, yet as a symbol of smartness it gave her a kind of distinction. It appeared to have fallen from the skies; it was put on in the wrong place, and it did not nestle, as it should do, and appear to grow out of her hair, since that glory of womanhood, in her case of a dull brown going slightly grey, was smooth, scarce and plainly

parted. Madame Fabrelle really would have looked her best in a cap of the fashion of the Sixties. But she could carry off anything; and some people said that she did.

Madame Frabelle's great gift is that of being wrong about everything. She is a monument to the failures of feminine intuition. She is an exciting store of inaccurate facts and false conjectures. She is the queen of nonsensical law-giving, masterfully inhabiting a very heaven of self-deception, as dotty as a horoscope. But people are charmed—again Miss Leverson's truthfulness—because Madame Frabelle is helplessly charmed by them. When she carries off Bruce, no one really minds. Two absurdities will have fulfilled themselves. Edith's excellences bored Bruce: he needed the dramatic companionship of a fellow self-deceiver.

Miss Leverson's admired males are too psychologically decorative: they are "connoisseurs of human nature", "urbane observers", "collectors of experience". They call Edith "*impayable*" when, frankly, she is really a moral coquette. But Miss Leverson's wit and perceptions are original. There are Lady Cannon's florid and massive clothes which, like her furniture, "express a violent, almost ominous conventionality, without the slightest touch of austerity to tone it down". Edith Ottley's appearance has "the rather insidious charm of somehow recalling the past while suggesting something undiscovered in the future". The random dialogue of parties turns, with hardly a pause, from the disturbing perception —"something in his suave manner of taking everything for granted seemed to make them know each other almost too quickly, and gave her an odd sort of self-consciousness"—to the hilariously vapid:

Captain Willis lowered his voice to a confidential tone and said:

"D'you know what I always say is—live and let live and let it go at that: what?"

"That's a dark saying."

"Have a burnt almond," said Captain Willis inconsequently as though it would help her to understand.

Writers of comedy have to bear as best they can the charge of triviality, in spite of the fact that their eye for detail and their instinct of selection give them an exceptional power to render the surface of life. How rarely do realists catch that surface. The other charge that they are evasive or, of all things, not "serious" is even more stupid, for they above all convey by their laughter the sense of danger that is inseparable from delight in the moment. In artificial comedy and the comedy of manners this sense of danger is intense. Miss Leverson lives by this. But the quality that has helped most to keep so much of her work in the perennial present is, quite simply, her feminine appetite for news:

> All women love news of whatever kind; even bad news gives them merely a feeling of pleasurable excitement . . .

Heavier novelists die off in a decade or two from a surfeit of information.

AN IRISH OBLOMOV

THERE is a terrifying sentence in James Stephens's account of his meeting with Joyce in Dublin that unfortunately came to my mind when I was struggling with Samuel Beckett's trilogy, *Molloy*; *Malone Dies*; *The Unnamable*—"I looked at him", says Stephens, "without a word in my mouth except vocabulary." Will someone not chart the vivid but interminable ocean of Irish garrulity for us, point out the shallows and the depths, tell us where the words are vocabulary only and where they connote ideas or things, where they are propitiatory magic, where egomania filling in time and place? Where is language used for language's sake, and where is it used as a gabble-gabble ritual to make tolerable the meaninglessness of life? It would be of practical help to know whether a writer was drowning well within his own depth or out of it; and when it would be decent to leave him to it—possibly coming back later, after a smoke, to see how he was getting on.

One does this with *Tristram Shandy*. One does it with *Finnegans Wake*. Pending necromantic guidance, with Beckett's novels, one does the same. They are lawsuits that never end, vexations, litigations joined with the tedium, the greyness, the grief, the fear, the rage, the clownishness, the physical miseries of old age where life is on the ebb, and nature stands by smiling idiotically. Why was I born, get me out of this, let me live on less and less, get me to the grave, the womb, the last door, dragging this ludicrous, feeble, windy broken old bag of pipes with me. Find me a hole. Give me deafness and blindness; chop off the gangrened leg; somewhere on this rubbish dump where I crawl there must be some final dustbin, where I can dribble, laugh, cry and maunder on the this and the that of the general mystery and occasionally give a toothless grin over an obscene word or a farcical sexual memory.

Flight, old age, and the wrangle about personal identity, these are Samuel Beckett's themes. A man is a vestige left to hop around in wearying argy-bargy after his invisible master: punishment, for the old, unremembered sin. Life is the *belle dame* with the mindless smirk and she hardly troubles to look at the victim who has been reduced to the total lethargy of compulsive speech. That is the joke: the mutilated thing can *talk*. In the first volume the man is Molloy, the tramp with crutches, a mixture of simplicity, hurt and lunatic energy. He can still spit with contempt at society:

> One of us at last! Green with anguish. A real little terrestrial! Choking in the chlorophyll. Hugging the slaughterhouse walls! Paltry priests of the irrepressible ephemeral!

He bashes along on his bicycle, through the town, trying to get to his mother. He runs over a dog—

> an ineptness all the more unpardonable as the dog, duly leashed, was not out on the road, but in on the pavement, docile at his mistress's heels. Precautions are like resolutions, to be taken with precaution. The lady must have thought she had left nothing to chance, so far as the safety of her dog was concerned, whereas in reality she was setting the whole system of nature at naught, no less surely than I myself with my insane demands for more light. But instead of grovelling in my turn, invoking my great age and infirmities, I made things worse by trying to run away. I was soon overtaken by a bloodthirsty mob of both sexes and all ages, for I caught a glimpse of white beards and little angel faces, and they were preparing to tear me to pieces.

—but the lady stopped them, saying she was taking the dog to the vet to be put down, in any case, and he had saved her a painful task.

This volume has all Beckett's headlong comic gift. Molloy is in the clownish state of senility, his disqualified life has the spirit either of a fairy tale or inverted idyll; and in his pestiferous search for "more light" on everything and nothing—mostly the latter—there is a grin half of mockery and half of frenzy on his scabby face. His sexual memories are funny because they are few, take him by surprise, and they are a mixture of the grotesque and touching, the dirty and the modest. He has dragged his body around all his life, and it follows him like some ignorant valet. There is far more to compare with *Tristram Shandy* in the caprices of this volume and its exploits in self-contradiction in order to hold the floor, than there is with Joyce.

In the second volume, *Malone Dies*, we move from the freedom of rebellion to loneliness. Malone, by the way, may be another aspect of Molloy; he doesn't know who he is. As far as I can make out the scene of the novel is a madhouse or infirmary for the old, and Beckett becomes the grammarian of solitude. The senses are dying. How does Malone know where the veils of air end and the prison walls begin? The body turns in smaller and smaller circles; the mind conjugates trifles. Here Beckett intervenes with some satirical observation of normal people, a trite couple and their favourite son, a piece which might have come out of Sartre's *Nausée*, or Nathalie Sarraute, and we are reminded that Beckett writes his novels first in French.

But we return to endless hair-splitting, metaphysical speculation sliding from association to association, and these convey that as age increases the tedium of life, so the unwearying little talker in the brain, with his lawsuit against life, bosses every half minute of it. Grief and pity hang between his words; but the book unexpectedly ends in wholesale murder, when the feeble-minded inmates of the infimary are taken out on a picnic.

In the third volume, Molloy, Malone, Mahood, Murphy —whatever the name now is—is a lump, almost sightless, stone deaf, always weeping, mutilated, immovable, the helpless centre of a world that he can be conscious of very rarely. He is about to become Worm, all human identity gone. The archaeological kind of critic who can recover a novel from its ruins may be able to make something of this volume. I find it unreadable, in the sense that I cannot move from paragraph to paragraph, from page to page. It is all significance and no content.

The stream of consciousness, so lively and going dramatically from image to image in Joyce, is here a stream of imageless verbosity occasionally broken by a jab of obscene anger, but grey, grey, and it goes monotonously along in phrases usually about seven words long, like some regularly bumping old tram. This is, of course, not so much the stream of consciousness as the stream of solitude and provides the comedy of overhearing a man talking to himself—Bloom, one recalls, rarely talked; things "came up" in his mind. He was in the midst of drama—a comedy that is genuine enough certainly, but not of boundless interest.

Why is Beckett interesting as a writer? As a contemporary phenomenon, he is one more negative protest against the world going to the slaughterhouse, one more protest on behalf of privacy, a voice for myopia. He is a modern Oblomov, fretful and apathetic, enclosed in private fantasy, dropping off into words instead of sleep. They are eloquent, cunning, unremitting words.

He is far from feeble, for there is a devil-like slyness in the half grin on the faces of his old men who can hit out with their crutches. What tedium! they exclaim—speaking not only of existence and human solitude—but, we suspect, of ourselves. His imagination has the Irish cruelty and self-destructiveness that Yeats once spoke of. Beckett's anti-novels, like all anti-novels, have to deal with small areas of experience because their pretension is to evoke the whole of life, *i.e.* life unfixed by art; the result is that these verbose books are like long ironical, stinging footnotes in small print to some theme not formulated. But there is a flash of deep insight in the madness he evokes: it is strange that in a generation which has put all its stress on youth and achievement, he alone should have written about old age, loneliness and decrepitude, a subject which arouses perhaps our deepest repressed guilt and fears. He is the product of a civilisation which has become suddenly old. He is a considerable, muttering, comic writer, and although he conveys unbearable pain, he also conveys the element of sardonic tenacity and danger that lies at the heart of the comic gift.

ALEXANDRIAN HOTHOUSE

IN France, Germany and in the United States, we are told, Mr Lawrence Durrell is now the most admired of British novelists. For ourselves, he is a mixture of traveller, poet and the brilliant raconteur in depth, of non-stop loquacity. Our literature grows blooms like this in the expatriate and Imperial hot-houses—Mr Durrell was planted in the Middle East and the Mediterranean—a Ouida as well as a Kipling, a Norman Douglas as well as a D. H. Lawrence; a Byron, but also a Disraeli and a Hichens.

Where our exotics excel is in a matchless sense of place which, I believe, is not approached by any literature in the world. Mr Durrell's evocation of Alexandria, in *Justine*, *Balthazar* and *Mountolive*, and now in *Clea*, is one of the finer mirages in our writing. It is an astonishing collection of fragments, a self-perpetuating generation of vivid pictorial illusions, obsessive, poetic, curious, scholarly, and headily at the mercy of mood and memory. This writing of his is splendid, even when the pedal is down, because the poetic image is the image of precision; and arresting, because contemporary English prose has either—in one of Durrell's phrases—got a hot potato in its mouth or has been nibbled close by the bleak teeth of modern criticism. In either case, it looks like rain. The writer whose subject is illusion—Mr Durrell's—is entitled to colour, image and fantasy and it is no good complaining that, on the subject of cities, he does not write like Smollett, who succeeded fearfully in a different way. Fragments stick:

> Streets that run back from the docks with their tattered, rotten supercargo of houses, breathing into each others' mouths, keeling over . . .
>
> the early spring dawn with its dense dew, sketched upon the silence that engulfs a whole city before the birds awaken it . . . the sweet voice of the blind muezzin hanging like a hair in the palm-cooled upper airs . . .
>
> in the summer the sea-damp lightly varnished the air. Everything lay under a coat of gum.

And there are the set pieces, like the sight of the desert at the meeting of the Copts or the duck-shoot in the delta. Or those long interiors: the cellar in which the child prostitutes come out by candlelight like a cloud of bats, or the Minister of the Interior's appalling reception-room, with the old, sugared and slothful spider pillowing his stomach on the divan.

But as a novelist? A novel can be anything; but, struggle as Mr Durrell does with his conviction that he is conducting an experiment in "the novel of sliding panels", or creating a mosaic of plot and symbol in layers and depths, he is really a raconteur, a master of the episode. He cannot stop. *Clea* appears to round off the Justine series, but in it he is clearly hankering after new twists and densities. In *Justine* he was all surface; in *Balthazar* he showed us it was a false surface; in *Mountolive*, the political novel which really rooted his characters, he got depth at last. I think this volume is the making of the quartet. But in *Clea*, invention and ingenuity have become a habit. The difficulty is that the war has come, the spell of old Alexandria and the decadent elation that sustained it have gone. There is no artifice to believe in. Pursewarden, who began to shape in *Mountolive*, lectures us for hours about sex, literature and the North in the only too-well-known voice of Norman Douglas. This is not the earlier, difficult Pursewarden of scandalous sexual misbehaviour, fighting the Foreign Office, and dumbfounding and seducing that honking, hysteric Lesbian, Justine; breaking the lock-jaw of her desire for martyrdom by making her laugh at herself for the first time in her life. In *Clea* poor Pursewarden, who has had to bear much from Mr Durrell, is given a guilty secret; he has committed incest. It is as solemn as the committal to the deep. It is made to sound like one of the seven deadly virtues. His smut is below standard, too.

And then, in *Clea*, those letters, diaries and mimicries which Mr Durrell has skilfully used to give a change of view to the earlier books, swamp the narrative. There is still good farce, which, after place, is one of Mr Durell's strong gifts. The saga of Scobie, the Catholic Police Chief with 'tendencies' (Eonism) gets broader after his death. This sinning and Cockney prowler, with a bad accent, is canonised as a Moslem saint by accident because of local popularity. His tomb contains his bath tub—no body available—and works miracles. There is Dr Amaril's romance with a girl for whom he makes an artificial nose, a charming tale; and more dreadful, the tale of Dr Balthazar's last love affair. In a panic because he is obliged to take to false teeth, and sees in this a sign of declining powers, the philosophical old dabbler in the Cabbala falls in love with a beastly young actor, and is driven to the most extravagant and pitiable humiliations of homosexual jealousy. He ends by attempting to cut off his own hands. (Hand symbols and hand-cutting occur more than once in Mr Durrell's quartet, for as he annotates the course of European sexual practice and fantasy from Rabelais to Sade, Sade gets most of the cheers. As a gesture to Home, there are two cheers for D. H. Lawrence.)

Mr Durrell's ingenious method of sliding the panel and showing us many episodes again with new and unexpected shadows, is dramatic and absorbing; it cannot disguise the fact that his leading people are not people at all. They are vehicles of events; they are a poet's notes; they are fables, subjects of one another's conversation and, in the case of the women, are seen only in the light of desire. It is Mr Durrell's point as an artist that they are fervid aspects of the city, created by its moments. They build up, of course, as time passes. Justine, the nymphomaniac, the banker's wife, the narrator's mistress, is shown first as a figure of mystery, then as a raucous hysteric and finally we get a real insight into her nature when we discover that she is diverting her desire to suffer into serious political plotting. Politics calm her sexually. She is the perpetual *intrigante* with a rage for power. When the plot fails she turns upon her husband and becomes not the mysterious holy whore, but the true married scold. So Justine acquires character—but only through the say-so of her lovers who observe her. She is less a woman than gossip. We see the rest of Mr Durrell's characters as we might see them in Casanova, almost only in their relation to some peculiarities of sexuality, its pleasures, pains, dissimulations, ironies and unpredictable turns.

Mr Durrell and his people are continually talking. They talk well and wittily, with instructed scepticism and an immense amount of quotation, including quite a few old intellectual gags, like Mommsen's about the Celts destroying civilisations and creating none of their own. It indeed often seems that loquacity has been substituted for sex. And *are* they talking about love? Not really; only about Narcissism and desire. Sterile, they are talking about its perversity, its sadness, its anecdotage, its variety, its passing. Their sexual love is easy, but after the sexual act there is still unsatisfied desire. Exhausted romantics, they are looking over the sleeping lover's shoulder. Love—and Mr Durrell as a good Mediterranean prides himself on his knowledge of its variety—rarely grows beyond that first stage in his novels. He speaks in Stendhalian phrase of *amour passion*, but does not give us an example of it. No one is possessed.

Here and there, there is a *glimpse* of love—and we have to grant that he sets out to be a novelist of fragmentation—as when, for example, in a very fine scene, an old man cries for his mistress on his death-bed in hospital. He is an old dealer, she is a cabaret dancer with many customers who has long ago left him. He wants her now, not for comfort, not to expose a broken heart, but to confess to her that he once or twice robbed her and cheated her. He wants to clear his conscience. Surely, love is the bloodstream of the moral nature; Mr Durrell sees human beings as thinned-out spirits off on some kind of erotic hunt who live only in the eyes and the senses, on the nerves, in expert pleasure and in terror. We accept this because he tells us we are in Alexandria, the androgynous, where people are "wounded in their sex"; but it knocks the bottom out of old Pursewarden as a sage. It is noticeable indeed that Mr Durrell's people acquire character when they are seen outside of love, especially the men. Narouz, the rich Copt and farmer, for example, who murders and is murdered, is far more real than his brother, the mysterious Nessim, the banker who is caught in Justine's affairs. Nessim becomes real only when we see him plotting to run arms into Palestine. Mountolive, the ambassador, becomes real when he is shocked out of his long day-dream of desire for Nessim's mother, is caught by political intrigue, and goes through the shocking and terrifying scene in the child's brothel.

If mutability and illusion are the subjects of this novelist who is afloat on fine words and an avidity for art and ideas, his means are shock, boldness and a mastery of intrigue, pattering and story-telling. His experiment in repeated rewritings succeeds to a great extent because the shift has some of the abruptness of the theatre in it. In all things he is an artist; even when he bores, he bores us as an artist by striking too many attitudes. When the shift fails it is because he relies excessively on long-winded narrators who are supposed to be new voices, but who are in fact as clever in the same way as he is. The influence of Norman Douglas and the desire to out-Juan *Don Juan* have been baneful. It produces Ouida. But one does not forget the absurdities of Scobie, the love life of Pombal, the French diplomat. One admires the caricature, the murder of Narouz, the scene in which Pursewarden fails to make love to Melissa, succeeds when he has confessed a secret to her, and drops her suddenly when she accidentally reveals a trivial yet deadly secret to him; one does not forget Scobie's death, the horror of the brothel—or anything which springs from intrigue. For intrigue buzzes out of Mr Durrell's tremendous power of observation and invention. His eyes are forever watching; his ears forever hearing. The Decadent palls, the compulsive talker goes on and on, but again and again the romantic inventor breaks through like a bursting flower. He is unlike any novelist we now have.

KIPLING'S SHORT STORIES

AFTER Dickens, Kipling is the only very considerable English writer of fiction to have been popular in the most popular sense and to excite the claim to genius. He might dabble in popular myth-making and put on the swank that goes with journalistic writing, but impurity had to be reckoned as in the nature of his bristling and generous gift. By 1910, the critical esteem had begun to go; for anyone who grew up in the 'twenties it had gone; when one looked at a page or two of Kipling in the 'thirties, he looked like a progenitor of The Thing we all hated. It was easy to tie his politics round his neck and sink him. Long after that, it was a shock (when we opened one of his books) to discover that his politics might not have been as important as we had made out; that his real themes were anterior and that he had an independent gaiety and authority in his sentences suggesting a much darker experience than the political. One was faced by a variable but continuous exhibition of musketry over an enormous terrain, which alerted the mind so long as he never allowed his own feelings, or those of his characters, to come out into the open, but left them to be guessed. He was, in any case, better at what was choked and strangled and, puritanically, admired pain. But, of course, he did not always leave us guessing; blatancy, emphasis, the breezy sentences beginning with a relative came back and, being sensitive, we put the book down and resumed our ignorance, preferring those writers who had grown up and who were not ashamed of the heart.

It is in this mixed state of prejudice, ignorance and unwillingness to go back to old topicality that I approach a subtle and partial critical study by Miss J. M. S. Tompkins, *The Art of Rudyard Kipling*. She invites one to enter a labyrinth and to trace the course of a genius she believes to be undeniable and which went on painfully growing until, in his later, complex and allusive work, it was purified and at its fullest. It is a little embarrassing, when one looks from her book into Kipling's tales, to find she is more sensitive than her subject was. The study does not claim to be comprehensive; startlingly but firmly, she leaves his politics out altogether. ("I was a child of the British Empire, as I am a subject of the British Commonwealth, and I have never found either position embarrassing. I regret that I shall not live long enough to see our humanly imperfect but undeniably great achievement of Empire fairly assessed in the long view of history.") This decision is not as damaging as it might sound, for she is not a biographer, nor a critic who runs the writer and the man together at every point. She is concerned only with the writer and, even there, most of all with the short stories. It is by these, she conveys, that what he did must be judged. To say that Kipling is the greatest English writer of short stories is to astonish oneself. He is—because no others before him made it expressly their *metier*.

Kipling's choice and aptitude are un-English; they are a little French; they are very American. If one were to raise political questions, one would say that Englishness was thrashed into him, that it was imposed. He invented myths for the sahibs, full of moral words, tribal signs and masonic grips, but the matter of his stories has often more in common with that of American predecessors like Twain, and successors like Hemingway and Faulkner, than it has with anything English writers have done. *Mary Postgate* is a foreigner's searching portrait of an English spinster. We cover that sort of thing up. The fantasy of *The Man who would be King* is a frontier story, a natural for Mark Twain—see the King and Duke episode in *Huckleberry Finn*—and the preoccupation with toughness, cunning and shrewdness, and above all with the testing of personality, is not restrained by our sociability, dignified by our severity of satire or confined to studies of character seen in its security. In fact, the common opinion is that Kipling failed precisely in character-drawing where traditional English novelists have succeeded. I do not think he felt much need to draw character; from his Anglo-Indian point of view he thought the islanders too set, smug and narrow. This would have to be the starting point of any discussion of his politics; he became an English patriot in a most un-English way—except for the sentimentality—not by rebellion from within but from a sense of grandeur from without, and from that sense of colonial superiority which always made Anglo-Indians an annoyance and a joke. But the theory of a crypto-American Kipling is mine; it is not Miss Tompkins's. Indeed, far from it. For her he is an Elizabethan:

> . . . a traditional writer with a traditional and recurrent cast of English temperament . . . he delighted in the Elizabethan dramatists. Man in a state of strong excitement stretched beyond his normal stature on the rack of anguish, passion, or his own will, was as much his theme as theirs though in him the will is stretched to service rather than to self-assertion. In Kipling, as in his elder brothers, the moral and sensational go hand in hand. Strain, the oppression and horror of melancholy throw up for him, as for them, eccentricities of behaviour which he observes with curiosity, and open up tracks of mental experience, of which he seeks to convey the strangeness. . . . Like the Elizabethans he had an original and unembarrassed love of eloquence . . . his danger, like theirs, was excess, the premature outbreak of the imagination into extravagant emphasis and unsupported hyperbole.

Kipling loved pattern, craftsmanship and the science of all trades. Yet the novel he could not master. Perhaps he had learned brevity too young; perhaps it was due to his facility as a poet; perhaps he burned up himself and his material too quickly or—as Mr Edmund Wilson suggested in *The Wound and the Bow*—failed to confront himself. Miss Tompkins thinks Kipling mastered the novel by relinquishing its form and became our unique short-story writer, and one of the greatest in all literatures, by straining into the short form the intense, highly charged essences of the longer one. He sought complexity as he sought discipline. The greater the material —*Mrs Bathurst*, for example, which covers the affections of a lifetime, trails across a Continent and ends in passion and horror—the more the essentials are reduced to a line or two, the quicker and more cunning the dodging among events and time. He proceeds, as a novelist does, less by narrative than by changing structure. We have seen Hardy reduce a novel to a dozen lines of verse. Kipling's dramatic cutting is more like Browning's, and the art of both writers lies in making us supply the missing scenes and often the most important one. Time is no difficulty for him. The setting he always gives us vehemently—after that, it is all fencing as if he were outmatching us, driving us into a corner, until we give in, and it is we who tell him, not he who tells us, what happened.

Kipling is not one of those short-story writers who settle on a mere aspect of a subject, a mood, an emotion or a life. He takes the whole subject and reduces it, in form, to the dramatic skeleton. Important issues are left obscure as if the author himself did not know what had happened or was trying to trade on mystery, and we often have to read back to see where we went wrong; yet the effect is of extent, panorama and crowded life. One explanation lies in Kipling's genius for conveying place and physical presence; the more important one is his triumph over what, as a novelist, would have been his failing: his incapacity to write of character in detail. What he tells us about people, what by a paradox makes them vivid, is that they belong to the common run; they are ordinary engineers, seamen, soldiers, housemaids, reliable villagers, conventional youths, Indians anonymous within their sects, occupations or races. They have no character; they have, simply, a fate; and it is this that evokes the presence of hundreds like them. Kipling is able to suggest that he has no life of his own but has lived by knowing all about such lives. He may be—he often is—too much of a know-all, swaggering shrewdly in and out with the low, the mean or the extravagant view, but this basic losing of himself and knowing is a powerful gift.

Miss Tompkins is aware that Kipling presents difficult problems of taste. The exaggeration, the sentimentality, the horseplay, are dealt with as best she can. I doubt whether his sentimentality can be discussed as a question of fashion: sentimentality—as distinct from sentiment—arises when we impose an idea upon a feeling in order to obscure it. Kipling is sentimental about duty, when he wishes to conceal his ambiguous feelings about suffering and cruelty. *Mary Postgate* is an unsentimental story because it does not evade the terrible fact that old Miss Postgate looked beautiful, attractive and satisfied when she had experienced a sadistic revenge. The most displeasing sentimentalities in Kipling relate to his guess-work magic and mysticism and they lead to mistakes in craftsmanship—the letter-box which sticks out like a gadget in the superb story of *The Wish House*. But in sketching out the map of Kipling's pilgrim's progress, from the period of brashness and hurt into the arenas of revenge, anger, healing, pity and the terror of illness, breakdown and the abyss, Miss Tompkins shows us a Kipling who is far less a trickster and far more a man deeply caught by injury, pain, hatred and the craving for purgation, and who uses every ounce of his experience. He had been born in the Methodist tradition and knew the burden is on the individual soul. It is also one of the splendid characteristics of Kipling as an artist that he can consider this burden disrespectfully, in jeering and fantastic terms, as well as in terms of mercy, pity, horror and resignation.

To make her point about the density of Kipling's art, Miss Tompkins makes a long and ingenious analysis of the baffling *Dayspring Mishandled.* Like many of the late stories it requires minute attention from the reader, but although it has all the marks of a master of building and technique, and although the theme of the emptiness and irrelevance that waits on a life-long scheme of revenge is a good one, the story seems to me an example of Kipling's vice of attitudinising in order to avoid the explicit. Miss Tompkins suggests it may be a story about the dangers of his own imaginative obsession with revenge and, in this sense, the tale has the interest of a piece of ingenious self-criticism. As a tale it is dim and esoteric; who and what poisoned whom with what? we ask. The later Kipling was a conjuror, not a mystifier like the later Henry James.

Mr Edmund Wilson has said that Kipling lacked faith in the artist's vocation and put the doers, makers and rulers of the day before the artist in esteem. This is true when we consider Kipling as a propagandist, and Miss Tompkins has purposely avoided that aspect of his work. At his best—*On Greenhow Hill*, *The Wish House*, *Love-o'-Women*, *The Gardener*, *The Man who would be King* or *The Bull that Thought*—the criticism misses. In this last tale, indeed, the artist is the explicit conqueror, and *The Man who would be King* can be read as farcical and deadly satire on the British in India. Kipling had the gaiety of the word in his veins and he saw himself as an artist through and through. What Mr Wilson may be getting at is Kipling's often showy and evasive pose of common sense, in which the average comes out on top; or that hard, no-nonsense grin on his face which flatters average human insensibility by calling it experience. Pain is over and over again his subject; so much so that he cannot evoke simple feeling without encasing it in bandages or see the fullness of love except in the perspective of its dire consequences.

He is indeed afraid of deep feeling in the foreground and the fear—perhaps because of his enormous gifts—leads him into stretches of middling vulgarity. But, in fact, Kipling grew out of clever journalism to have the strongest feeling for the means of art and all the artist's deference to difficulty. He can even be said to have had this feeling exorbitantly; but given the man he was and his populous mind, it is what made him our prolific and unique writer of short stories. The art thrives on personal limitations.

EL CID

UNTIL fifty years ago our interest in the great epic heroes was literary and nothing else. Figures like Arthur, Roland, the Cid and many others, had been revived by the Romantic movement and were charged by its taste for hero-worship and history. So slight was their relationship with anything going on in the world in the nineteenth century, that the interest in them looks like an attempt to escape from a grey mercantile present into a glamorous past. It was not entirely that; there were the psychological sympathies of the power-lovers, the hankerings after the superman in the Victorian age, the desire to reduce the hero to the outstanding bourgeois. And there were occasional emotional rebounds as well. Southey's superb translation of *The Chronicles of the Cid* may have owed something to emotions stirred by the citizens of the Revolution or the figure of Napoleon, as well as to the dramatic personal contact with Spain. Yet all these responses remain literary and even antiquarian, and some readers must have felt, as I very often have, that the epic heroes were epic bores of featureless and exhausting simplicity.

Times have changed. The conditions out of which a living epic literature might arise have appeared in many parts of the world. Not in the West, perhaps, but certainly in Continents where there has been continuous war, and where new orders are forming themselves. We have seen popular movements give a legendary character to their leaders. We have seen leaders looking about them for useful myths. Myth-like figures bob up continually in popular culture. They do not last, for one eclipses another. But the myth-making faculty has generally revived, is no longer derided, is eagerly studied and is made to serve the ends of government—political, religious and psychological. We are back at a moment when a magic, like the discovery of the bones of St James at Compostela, is firmly exploited. In this climate the epic heroes come closer to us and we can see their roots in life. A book like Mr W. S. Merwin's translation of the *Poem of the Cid* has now an extra dimension, and since Southey wrote, the Cid has been liberated by that great Spanish scholar Ramón Menéndez Pidal. The Champion now stands clearly and firmly on the dusty soil of Castile and we can know for what solid reasons he became the legendary national hero, and why one of the impulses behind the writing of the poem was what we would now call propaganda. We can see a myth being used, and why it was used.

Rodrigo Diaz, the Cid or Lord, as the Moors called him, the Champion as he was called by the Castilians, was born in 1045 in the village of Vivar in the cornlands near Burgos. He died fifty-six years later in Valencia and the *Poem* of his real or fantastic feats was written forty years after his death by a Mozarábe (*i.e.*, a Christian born under Moorish rule) who may have known him. Many who knew him must have still been alive. Vivar was a frontier town. As a boy the Cid fought in the frontier wars of Navarre, and he was brought up at court. He could write. He came of noble stock, though not of the highest nobility, a matter of great importance and strong resentment in his life. The effect of the endless wars had been to increase the number of lesser nobility, the men who had horsemen and vassals, and the Cid belonged to this group. In Navarre whole populations became armigerous. They had their property in land and mills. (The Cid was mocked for his mills.) Their road to great wealth was to obtain the spoils of war and here the Cid enormously succeeded. His "ill-shod outcasts" told the Court of Barcelona: "We keep alive by taking from you and others." The prodigious loot obtained by him from his enemies turned him into a type of self-made millionaire whose daughters are sought for their money by the high nobility, but who, like their father, are socially despised. The *Poem* brings out strongly the private pride in something like a democratic attitude to life which was the great strength of the spirit of Castile, and which made that kingdom, and not feudal Leon, the leader in the wars of Reconquest and the most powerful of the Spanish states. The *Poem* is, in this sense, the voice of an unconscious wartime revolution.

The Cid has often been described as a freebooter, a soldier of fortune who sold himself to Moors and Christians, according to where the profit lay. This is not at all what he would have seemed to his contemporaries. At his birth, Christian Spain lay in the north, Moslem Spain in the south and east; but the majority of Spanish Moslems were, after three hundred years, of Ibero-Roman or Gothic stock. There was a mingling of races which had been made possible by Islamic rationalism. The people were bi-lingual. The Cid appears at the moment when a Moorish dynasty was weakening and becoming more penetrable by guerillas who could capture castles if they could not gain territory, and when many Moors had become vassals of the Christian north. In the eleventh century it was not astonishing that a Moorish king should entrust the government of his land to the Cid, nor that the Cid should fight for the Moorish Emir of Saragossa against the Count of Barcelona, nor that he should at other times extend Moorish lands at the expense of Aragon and Castile. The strange thing is that his loyalty to his own king, who had banished him and wronged him out of personal envy and perhaps because of the intrigue of the great landowners and high nobility of Burgos, was constant.

Slaughter and booty are the trades of the Cid. One of the famous moments of the poem occurs after the siege of Valencia where he takes his frightened wife up to the top of a tower so that she can watch the battle and "see how they earn their bread". In its terse, plain, homely, always concrete fashion, the poem sets out the labours of an astute fighting man's life, in the sense that he is earning his living and doing what he wishes with his own. Religion is there, but hardly more than formally recognised. There is little of the ideological crusader in him. He is a generous conqueror. There is frequent stress on his legal rights. He insists at the court on every tittle of them but always bows to the law himself. The amusing and well-known episode of borrowing money from the Jews on a false security—the boxes of sand said to be boxes of gold—indicates that the writer of the poem was aware of the economics of guerilla warfare and knew all about calling on bankers and arranging for commission. This plainness about the ordinary things of a country dealer's life, and the charming small touches—the little girl of nine who explains to the Cid that her family cannot allow a banished man into the house—set the hero in a recognisable world that he loves, and as a man to be esteemed. His pain at parting from his wife is not written up, but is thought of as an excruciating physical pain, in the traditional manner of Spanish realism:

> "now we part; God knows
>   when we shall come together"
> Weeping from his eyes
>   you have never seen such grief
> Thus parted the one from the others
>   as the nail from the flesh.

He is a real man among real things even when his exploits are fantastic:

> There the rout began
>   as it pleased God.
> My Cid and his Knights
>   rode in pursuit;

> You would have seen so many tent cords
> snapped, and the poles down,
> And so many embroidered tents lying on the
> ground.

And in the court brawl where the Cid storms at the rich nobles who have married his daughters and then left them stripped and beaten in a wood because they are not good enough socially, the scene has the roughness of nature. Here, above all, one sees the Cid quietly affirming the law. He is not a lawless man.

This plain, bare, directness of the *Poem*, its lack of hyperbole and of elaborate message, are in themselves delightful, but there is another aspect in which we see the myth-making faculty at work. Brenan discusses this in his *Literature of the Spanish People* and it can be followed in more detail in Pidal. The *Poem of the Cid* was written directly under the influence of the *Chanson de Roland*, which commemorated the greatness of Charlemagne three hundred years after his death, whereas the *Poem of the Cid* was almost contemporary. The *Chanson* has a quality, Brenan says, peculiar to French art but never found in Spanish. It does not stop at telling a story, "it sets up a universal pattern or example. Already in this period we can see the French mind at work, consciously and deliberately creating ideas and values." It is a work animated by the crusading spirit and fortified by national and religious propaganda; for it was the French, and especially the Benedictines of Cluny, the intellectual commissars of Europe, who had established the figure of St James of Compostela as a symbol of the Christian drive against Islam, and who had established the pilgrimage route across the Pyrenees to the shrine as a sort of political duty. The famous battle at Roncesvalles occurs on the prilgrims' road over the Pyrenees and is an incident in ideological warfare.

But as the Spaniards fought back against a real occupation

of their country, they began to resist the centralising sophisticated ambitions of a remote French Europe. The Spanish peasant disliked the new feudal tenures the Cluniac monks sought to impose. There was strong opposition to the introduction of the Roman rite. The Cid's handwriting itself is in the old script, not the new standard script being introduced by the planners of the new Europe. The *Poem of the Cid* is, in short, the assertion of the Spanishness of the struggle. The Cid is more than a great fighter, he represents the appearance of a Spanish view, opposed to the spirit of the French propagandists. Brenan says there is nothing in French literature of the twelfth century to compare with the assured and responsible political feeling of the *Poem of the Cid* and that one of the reasons for this was that the Spaniards were not taken up with the international question of the relations of the Church to the civil authorities. There was no ideological right and wrong for the Spaniards; on the contrary, from the simple view of the ordinary free man, the tone is set by that famous line: "God, what a good vassal, if only he had a good lord." If we are to look for a contemporary parallel—admittedly a dangerous amusement—we see the Spanish relation to the new monolithic system of France and Rome as something like, say, the relation of Yugoslavs to Russians. The situation is as primitive. The other point is that heroes may rise spontaneously, but they are not heroes unless they arise out of fundamental situations in their age—they are not merely courageous, fortunate men or splendidly tragic men—and that no myth crystallises about these popular figures except through the means of an acceptable propaganda. The French genius had to suggest an idea; the Spanish genius, to be effective politically, had to turn to a man and to convey that Islam was conquered and Europe saved, not by a complex organisation and an ideology, but by a banished man of just instincts, well-set in his own land.

MR FORSTER'S BIRTHDAY

"MAY I never resemble M. de Lesseps", E. M. Forster wrote when he considered the famous statue by the Suez Canal on one of his journeys to India. "May no achievement upon an imposing scale be mine." He has indeed been a haunting absence in the English novel, but on the occasion of his eightieth birthday, we can allow ourselves to dress up our prose in the boater and blazer of 1905 and think of his silence, since *Passage to India*, as "a rotten business", without a moral —like Harold's dropping of the oars and dying, in *The Point of It*—and of Forster's survival in our literature as a "cert". How does one survive if one does not impose? Forster has survived so far by interposing. Where his elders, Shaw, Wells, Kipling, imposed by sheer efficiency and manpower, Forster has interposed and influenced by a misleading slackness, by the refusal to speak in a public voice. This has given the personal a startling strength. He has had, one guesses, more influence on the educated middle-classes than any other English writer in the last thirty or forty years; for it is he who has taught them to disengage themselves from their inherited official, not to say imperial, personality. The Empire Kipling celebrated, Forster destroyed, and by a handful of out-of-date novels—for it was his fate to have a great deal of his material pulled from under his feet by the 1914 war. In saying his say against imperialism, he exhausted in advance what he could have said, as a novelist, against totalitarianism. He was kind enough to write articles.

One can rely on English life to produce these personal voices: a Samuel Butler, a Mary Kingsley, a Forster; in our own generation, a George Orwell. Their voices are direct, natural, distinct and disengaged, malignly flat. The machine stops when they start talking. We are so used to various sorts of "side" in English life, that we are startled and pleased by the note of authority from nature. Outside of our poetry we find that voice hard to hit on. Forster's gift has been just that: the private voice, carrying without effort, in the public place. The refusal to be great; the attack on the will and the bad heart; the two cheers instead of the usual three for democracy, the third being reserved for "love the Beloved Republic, which feeds upon Freedom and lives"; the belief in personal relationships—"the heart signs no document"—and an aristocracy of "the sensitives, the considerate and the plucky"; the debating-point plea for a "period of apathy, inertia and uninventiveness" —these are not withdrawals. Some are principled assertions of the supreme value of individual life; some are there to redress a balance. None is a brilliant paradox put down by a consuming brain. The apologist for softness is intellectually hard; the liberal who has been forced out of economic *laisser faire* and who believes that, nevertheless, *laisser faire* is the only doctrine that "pays"—a favourite ironic word—in the world of the spirit, is not proposing to let us do what we like. No one is let off in Forster's novels; like Jane Austen, he is a moral realist. Leonard Bast, the prototype of the angry young man, will get a rap on the knuckles for being a crushed soul. Having a chip —a maiden aunt seems to say—is no excuse for hysteria and making messes. Mr Wilcox catches it for being a soul-crusher. No tears, I seem to remember, are shed in Forster's novels. The sins of the heart, the failure to "connect", don't pay: they end in emptiness and panic. Those are better words than the jargon we have learned to use since the nervous breakdown, if only because they imply the moral imperative which is necessarily lacking in scientific studies of the mind.

There is the voice of the decided moralist in Forster; fortunately for the English novel, it has been transposed into the accents of the brusque and off-hand sanity which is in the central tradition of our comedy. Like Shaw's—though in the private interest, being more concerned with intimate feeling than with justice—Forster's is a comedy of ideas, and the danger there was that it would be expressed in a comedy of types or that he would have chosen people possessed of too great as kill in debate. He escaped this danger by his brilliant use of people who had been thoroughly unfitted to deal with their situations; like so many of Henry James's characters they are null or dull. Looking again at the early short stories which try out the themes to be taken up by *Where Angels Fear to Tread* or *Howards End* one is, at first, shaken by their pedestrian characters. How faded the people are now; they were born faded. Everyone outside Cambridge, one suspects, had to bear that accusation. Pompous, shabby, fussy suburbans they are, a collection of dim widows, daughters genteel or bossy, sons emasculated or emotionally congested. There are the mild, mechanical soldiers and all are liable to the blood-pressure, the wilfulness or the frostbite of a class-consciousness that has passed out of our knowledge. Formidable to deal with, these injured families are in danger of suffering (as Gissing's characters do) from an initial social pathos which is unforgivable in works of art. (Class theories play the part of the famous pathetic fallacy.) But, at second glance, the pathos goes. For these unlikely dullards are suddenly shaken by issues that had never occurred to them as existing; they are tripped up by melodrama, and their dullness makes their situation more arresting. They are made to skip and look lively. Mr Forster's beliefs are gentle, but he has no sentimental indulgence for weakness, and we remember that behind the fineness of his spiritual scrutiny lie the scrupulous traditions of the Clapham Sect; working in him is a spirited agnosticism and he does not see why the moral stakes for these muddled gamblers should not be put very high or why the upper middle classes should not have to risk all. In a way, he treats the English as if they were foreigners—a good idea considering how anti-foreign we have always been. His people swing between two states of mind—the disinterested and the benighted; and they fall into four foreign groups: the Teutonic, heading towards suicide in a sea of general ideas; his Latins—vulgar, avaricious but redeemable because they have not been castrated by good taste, are in the sink-or-swim of the instinctive life, and are liable to racial memories of Mediterranean paganism; the Oriental—passive, touchy and affronted; and the inhabitants of Tonbridge. Where have we seen the Forster situations before? In the novel-poems of the poet Clough, but whereas Clough is torn in half and is half-guilty, half-aggressive about his passivity and his escape into abstract thought, Forster presents the picture of a united personality who knows his mind. He knows what he is committed to.

It is not like the committal of Shaw or Butler—with whom he has, however, some affinity—nor any of the other committals of those who attacked the official late Victorian or Edwardian personality. His comedy is not freakish; it is not accommodating; there is no comfort in his scepticism. He is not scabrous and not at all the satirist, even if he caricatures; he is without the orgiastic sense of the full comic writers who revel in meaninglessness. He is not very sociable. His comedy is positive and spiritual; it has one most alarming trait: assurance. It is lonely. It has courage. He has always got his deadliest effect from a pretence of soppiness, from a casual, slangy disregard of the spirit of composure, or from a piece of parenthetical bathos. That opening argument about the cow in *The Longest Journey* is an example. If he is casually disrespectful, he is also casually abrupt about matters of life and death: the echo in the cave, Gino's outbreak of physical cruelty at the crux of sorrow in his child's death, young Wilcox getting three years for hitting someone with an old sword, Leonard dying perfunctorily because a bookcase falls on him, the baby falling out of the carriage, and those brief, dismissed sudden deaths in boats, playing fields and at the level-crossing. The intellectual must face causality; but he had better remember casualty and the inexplicable. None of these famous incidents will "do" in a realistic novel; the shock is too great and one might attack them as pointers to a suspicion that Mr Forster has exaggerated the device of not belonging to the world, and even that he grew up so quickly because he refused to join it. But these incidents, of course, succeed in romance where the writer has the licence to load his dice as he wishes. He has, also, a hankering after the pagan acceptance of mercilessness and the absence of tears.

Since his time, anyone in the nature of a personage has vanished from the English and American novel. The official has gone. The conversational, the vernacular voice has come in, but only in the interests of naturalism. It is common now to read novels in which physical life is rendered so clearly that we have the impression of seeing it before our eyes like the pebbles of a clear running stream. That impression can be had from Mr Forster's novels also—but with an important difference. It is the moral life that has the pebble-like clarity in *his* writing; he has made it tangible and visible. He has, so to say, speeded up the process of contemplation by making it clear what, in his view, needed to be contemplated. The plain conversational style is truly conversational in the sense that we feel several people are talking and trying to find out; in spite of James's influence, there is no sense of monologue. Forster's talk, like all good talk, has the quality of surprise.

It is easy enough to demonstrate that Forster represents the end of something. He has almost said so himself, though not quite: civilisations are a string of intermissions in the anger of time. He speaks at the end of liberal culture and, since there is no other, there is no implicit accusation. He agrees that this firm attachment owes something to privilege and we all know the dogma that, in its penultimate phase, a culture sees spiritual order in art alone; in its ultimate post-Forsterian phase it crumbles into a sort of Byzantine pedantry.

Forster's contribution to our present collective society is the reminder that it will be an arid and destroying desert if we remove the oasis of private life. But he is a dangerous master. All very well for him to refuse to be great: he had to fight the portentous. Educated and inured by the powerful, he was free to develop apathy and softness as an unexpectedly useful muscle. He had something pretty unscrupulous to disbelieve in. Does he feel, now, the burden peculiar to famous old age, that an age has caught up with him? Does he feel that, in England at any rate, a younger generation is carrying the cult of privacy and personal relationships to the lengths of whimsicality and eccentricity? It often strikes one that far too large a portion of educated energy is going into running England as a kind of private joke, an ingenious personal crossword. We are more gentle with one another, but we spend an inordinate amount of time being gentle; we are bathed to the point of sleep in tolerance and understanding. Forsterian teaching has been taken on without our recognising that it had the virility of a reaction. It is very pleasant to relax, as he taught us, and to believe (for example) in his notion that the bucket drops down into the unconscious and brings up the substance of the work of art. It is true. But isn't it Mr Forster's old enemy, the will, that has turned the handle and let the bucket down? It is a mistake to take this infertile and original writer literally. Thus his "apathy" really means "integrity". One other writer of his generation, Boris Pasternak, has it, and has demonstrated its phenomenal spiritual strength. Like him, Forster hands back the ticket, bored by the verbosity of the strong-willed, knowing that there is a creative force in the secrets of life. He is fresh because he is unable to conceive of a life without free choice; perhaps we would think him more than courageous, and actually great, if his novels had conveyed the other half of the argument: that we have to choose for others and that choice is made by others for us. But this is to ask for an inrush of ungoverned emotion beyond the scope of comedy.

PAIN AND WILLIAM GOLDING

THE essence of the novelist's art—especially the English novelist's—is the quotidian. From the moment Crusoe domesticates and diarises his desert island, the novel reflects the confidence the individual derives from the society he lives in. The risks of romance are gone; he is safe in the realist's nest: Selkirk was lonely, but Crusoe is the least lonely man in the world. This confidence has lasted in our tradition. But when we look up from our books into the life around us to-day, we wonder how the prosaic observer in realistic fiction can be so certain of himself. The quotidian art goes on describing and describing and, as far as externals are concerned, we cannot complain that the modern realist fails to describe the features of a changing, violent or collapsing society. But he is the spectator, in some lucky way insured and untouched; rarely does the novelist find the point at which we are involved or committed; rarely does he touch the quick, so that for once the modern alibi—"it is beyond the power of the imagination to grasp, etc., etc."—does not work. The imagination will never grasp until it is awakened; and facts will not awaken it. They merely strengthen opinion; and there is nothing so apt to shut us off from the world as the correct opinion about it. The imagination can be awakened only by the imagination, by the artist who has the power to break us down until the point of secret complicity is reached. It was this point which the writer of romance, undeterred by the day's events, and lost in his world of dramatic wishes, once knew how to reach.

Mr William Golding is an artist of this kind. His first three books, *Lord of the Flies* (1954), *The Inheritors* (1955) and *Pincher Martin* (1956) are romance in the austere sense of the term. They take the leap from the probable to the possible. *Lord of the Flies* has a strong pedigree: island literature from Crusoe to *Coral Island*, *Orphan Island* and *High Wind in Jamaica*. All romance breaks with the realistic novelist's certainties and exposes the characters to transcendent and testing dangers. But Golding does more than break; he bashes, by the power of his overwhelming sense of the detail of the physical world. He is the most original of our contemporaries. Many writers have been concerned, as a matter of argument, with what is rhetorically called "the dilemma of modern man", and have given us, as it were, lantern slide lectures on the anarchy of a poisoned future; they are really essayists sitting in comfort. Golding, on the contrary, scarcely uses an argument or issues a warning. He simply shakes us until we feel in our bones the perennial agony of our species. By their nature, his subjects—prep-school boys on a desert island in a world war, the calvary of a sailor who gave the right order but whose half-conscious body is being washed about the gullies of an Atlantic rock, the conflicts of a handful of Neanderthalers—could easily become the pasteboard jigsaw of allegory, pleasing our taste for satire and ingenuity; but the pressure of feeling drives allegory out of the foreground of his stories. He is a writer of intense visual gift, with an overpowering sense of nature and an extraordinary perception of man as a physical being in a physical world, torn between a primitive inheritance and the glimmer of an evolving mind. A dramatic writer and familiar with the strong emotions that go with the instinct of self-preservation—blind love for his kind, hatred, fear and elation—he is without hysteria. He is not cooking up freakish and exotic incident; he is not making large proclamations about man against nature, God, destiny and so on; he is seriously and in precise, individual instances gripped—as if against his will—by the sight of the slow and agonising accretion of a mind and a civilised will in one or two men, struggling against their tendency to slip back, through passion or folly, and lose their skills in panic. And there is pity for the pain they feel.

Pain is the essence of Mr Golding's subject. In *The Inheritors* it is the obscure pain of a baffled and dying group of ape men who see themselves surplanted by the more skilful new being called Man. The ape man experiences the pain of the grunt, of trying to communicate from one poor mind to another—"I have a picture. Can you see my picture?"—and also the pain of trying to distinguish, for a moment, what is inside from what is outside himself. From his tree he sees Man who is not afraid of water, as he is, who gets drunk on honey, who has invented love-play; he sees with a kind of grieving as an animal might grieve. In *Pincher Martin*, the tale of a modern sailor whose broken body is washed about the Atlantic rock, who eats limpets, is poisoned by his store of food and who eventually goes mad and dies, the pain is in the fight against physical hurt and loss of consciousness, in the struggle to put his educated will against his terrors. It is also in the Job-like protest against a defeat which wrongs everything he has believed in. In *Lord of the Flies*—the first and, I think, the best of these books—a group of schoolboys reenact the *Coral Island* story and the pain is in the struggle between the boys who revert through fear to the primitive and turn into savage hunters, and those who are trying vainly to preserve foresight and order. In the end, the boys are rescued, but not before they have lived through the modern political nightmare.

Mr Golding's sensibility to pain is the spring of his imagination and if, in all three stories, the heroes are smashed up, he is by no means a morbid or sadistic writer. The chest of the creature, running in terror from its enemies, scorches, the calves cramp, the skin tears, the body has to endure what animal panic lets it in for. Pain is simply the whole condition of man; it is the sign that he is awake and struggling with his nature, and especially with the terror which so suddenly scatters the mind. *Lord of the Flies* contains one episode of great horror. The rotting body of a dead parachutist is blown across the island in the night, almost stepping on the trees and the beaches, until it is taken out to sea. The sight is the final and clinching argument to the very young boys that a devouring Beast has really been among them; and one might conclude that this is a decisive symbol of human defeat and the meaninglessness of the struggle. The idea is irrelevant. Mr Golding's imagination is heroic. Against the flies that buzz round the dangling scarecrow must be put the elation of the adventure, the love of natural life, the curiosity of the eye, that run through the writing. And the compassion.

It is natural to compare *Lord of the Flies* with *Coral Island* —and then with *High Wind in Jamaica.* In *Coral Island* we see the safe community. A century without war and with a settled sense of the human personality has produced it. In Richard Hughes's book, we saw the first sign of disintegration: the psychologists have discovered that children are not small fanciful adults, but are a cut-off, savage race. In *Lord of the Flies* we understand that the children are not cut-off; anthropology, the science of how people live together, not separately, reflects the concern of the modern world which has seen its communities destroyed. The children in *Lord of the Flies* simply re-enact the adult, communal drama and by their easy access to the primitive, show how adult communities can break up. Of course, Mr Golding's improbable romances remain improbable; they are narrow and possible. The modern romancer has the uncluttered chance of going straight to the alienation of the individual and to the personal solitude that is one of the forgotten subjects. In our world, which is so closely organised we are hardly aware of what we are privately up to. We use large words like calamity, disaster, racial suicide, devastation; they are meaningless to us until an artist appears who is gifted enough to identify himself with a precise body being washed up against a precise collection of rocks, a precise being sniffing the night air for his enemy or feeling the full force of a particular blow. Until then, we are muffled in our alibi: "the imagination cannot grasp".

Lord of the Flies is the most accomplished of Mr Golding's novels. Its portraits of the shipwrecked boys and its understanding of them are touching and delightful and he is master of a rich range of scene and action. In this book his spirit and his serenity are classical. *Pincher Martin* is more chock-a-block, but it has fine descriptions of the roaring, sucking deafening sea scene on the rock which we know stone by stone. He is a modern writer here in that his eyes are pressed close to the object, so that each thing is enormously magnified. We see how much a man is enclosed by his own eyes. The important quality of all Golding's descriptions is that they are descriptions of movement and continuous change and are marked by brilliant epithets. (One remembers: "three prudish anemones".) There is this picture of the swimming sailor, almost at the rock:

> Ropes held him, slipped and let him go. He saw light, got a mouthful of air and foam. He glimpsed a riven rock face with trees of spray growing up it and the sight of this rock floating in mid-Atlantic was so dreadful that he wasted his air by screaming as if it had been a wild beast. He went under in a green calm, then up and was thrust sideways. The sea no longer played with him. It stayed its wild movement and held him gently, carried him with delicate and careful motion like a retriever with a bird. Hard things touched him about the feet and knees. The

> sea laid him down gently and retreated. There were hard things touching his face and chest, the side of his forehead. The sea came back and fawned round his face, licked him. He thought movements that did not happen. The sea came back and he thought the movements again and this time they happened because the sea took most of his weight. They moved him forward over the hard things. Each wave and each movement moved him forward. He felt the sea run down to smell at his feet then come back and nuzzle under his arm.

But this book succeeds less when it takes us into the sailor's chaotic recollections of his life. It contains some flashes back to scenes of jealousy and rivalry which are hard to grasp. It may be that Golding's sense of theatre—often strong in writers of romance—has overcome him here. (He is the author of a witty satirical play, *The Brass Butterfly*, which is excellent reading.) But in making us feel in the current in the modern world, instead of being stranded and deadened by it; in providing us with secret parables; in unveiling important parts of the contemporary anguish and making them heroic, knowable and imaginable, he is unique.

GRUB STREET

"GISSING: the English Gorki with a butterfly collar," says Mr G. W. Stonier in his introduction to *New Grub Street*. Moscow, transmuted, becomes Camberwell and is lamed. It is as well to remember the Russian quality of our very suburban novelist for, like Meredith and Disraeli, Gissing brings an alien's or exile's unconventional insight into English society. They are all self-created foreigners: Disraeli, the Jew; Meredith with his German education and his Welsh illusions; Gissing living abroad in dreams of Renaissance man and the Greek classics while he listens to the Museum cough in the Reading Room of Great Russell Street. (A scholar, Gissing must be one of our few novelists who is also a linguist; he spoke French perfectly, read German and Italian easily, beside the classical tongues. He knew some Spanish and attempted Russian.) One sees what moods and material the English novel has lost in being written by Englishmen; that is to say, by those Englishmen who, in Mr Stonier's good phrase, could "only dramatise their own self-satisfactions". And we recall that the great Russian novels of the nineteenth century arose from the failure of a class, whereas the English sprang out of its success.

Gissing's failure and his exile are the cause of his fame. We are driven back, as always with imperfect artists, to the entanglement of the person and his work. As Mr Walter Allen has pointedly said in *The English Novel* the fiction of Gissing is "too personal, the powerful expression of a grudge". No other English novelist until then had had a chip the size of Gissing's; self-pitying, spiritless, resentful, humourless, his lucid bleat drags down his characters and his words. There is a disturbing complacency in him as he stands at the sink and tells us that life is wretched and defeating, and many an indignant reader must have felt that Gissing was myopic. Like the young Jasper Milvain in *New Grub Street* he seems to raise his chin and talk to the upper air when talking about himself. And then, like many men whose life is shut in by unbelievable domestic wretchedness, Gissing was self-centred and did not recognise that, if one is going in for this sort of thing, one had better open one's eyes and recognise that life is not merely dreary and miserable; it is savagely cruel and utterly appalling. Gissing wrote less of the horror he knew than of the apathy which it engendered. He writes as if he were a mere effect. To return to Mr Stonier:

> One need only lose oneself in London or in the similar streets of any large town, to experience the monotony of anguish uppermost in Gissing. He respects the low affront, not hurrying, in imagination, to overpaint it with bright colours; the life behind windows does not grow comic or enormous; distance lends no enchantment, and no music steals up the gutters to transform what is into what is not. He lacks the fairy or imp of entertainment; but as the bias of fiction-writing goes, that is not such a disadvantage. He cannot help seeing plain, being faithful, taking the bad tooth into account.

Gissing is very Russian in his overpowering sense of the stale and unoccupied hours we have to lug around with us and this is his peculiar importation into the English novel.

Today, Mr Walter Allen's suggestion of the grudge is more interesting. In some ways the grudge of several of our young novelists resembles Gissing's, as if Gissing were their perverse prophet and progenitor. There are hints of it in all his work and it is particularly strong in *New Grub Street*. The grudge is concerned with education and opportunity. It has two aspects. Why pass an Education Act, giving clever Board School boys the chance to become cultivated men when they will only find themselves in stultifying and unseemly surroundings and without the means to live in some accord with their minds; and why educate ordinary boys so that they can become the customers for everything that is vulgar and trivial in popular, commercial culture? When Gissing wrote *New Grub Street*, the new journalism with its obsession with things like "What the Queen Eats" was showing its first signs. Now, it is easy to show that either the competitive instinct or the reforming spirit of social conscience—both of which Gissing lacked—were required of the clever Board School boy in return for his privilege. Gissing resented that only the rich could join the Past. For the unclever, Gissing had somehow got the idea (as Mr Walter Allen says) that the aim of education was merely to teach people to read books. He was the scornful scholarship winner. (He appears to make one exception in his dislike of the new journalism; in its higher forms of popularisation it educates women. One recognises here the man who suffered from the tongues of ignorant viragoes.)

The grudge of Gissing is the grudge of the outsider. He shows the psychological characteristics in his attitude to the prostitute and the servant girl he married. The violence in these vicious women is really matched, not by the passivity of his temperament, but by what one suspects to be the isolation and ruthlessness of his own mind. Morley Roberts, in his disguised biography of Gissing, *The Private Life of Henry Maitland*, happily reissued in 1958 with a key, by Richards Press, believed that Gissing simply desired the whole sex and, in his self-imposed loneliness and incapable of love, thought anyone would do. One has the horrible suspicion that he felt punishment justified him and so set him free. But—to get on more certain ground—Gissing was an outsider in rejecting modern society altogether because it did not provide a place for the recalcitrant scholar and the pure artist who was poor. The theme of *New Grub Street* is the tragedy of the intellectual worker. The book is a full conspectus of the literary situation done with Gissing's grey exactitude and clarity. The vulgar comic view of writers as a collection of eccentrics is dropped; he catches their fundamental dignity, anxiety and egotism. It is bad enough to be an artist, with its appalling gift of self-knowledge, without being obliged to kill the love of your wife, slave till you are blind, and end ill, half-starved and counting the pennies, behind the tightly drawn curtains of lower-middle-class respectability. The portrait of the wretched, gifted and only moderately saleable Reardon in this book is masterly, for Gissing is unremitting in observation. Without money, a James or a Shaw would just as certainly go down to the smell of last night's dinner in the seedy backroom. Gissing's simple description of the writer's day as he sits at his desk is exact, touching and terrifying; one feels half-elated, half-sickened at the end of it. For, allowing for one deficiency in Reardon's character, the morbid lack of will, the portrait would serve for any novelist.

Those who have the grudge nowadays have, of course, no interest in Gissing's concept of the artist or in his belief in the culture he belongs to. All the same, the conditions of literary society have not changed much since Gissing's times. Journalism, with its short-term shots of success, its weekly injec tion, still offers its therapy to the writer who can stand the ulcers and suicidal depressions of creative writing no more. Inflation and high taxation have wiped out the rewards of the successful and have reduced the less successful to the role of commentators frantic for a new slant. Our society will reward highly any writer who agrees to compound on his gifts and abandon them. A creative writer must have time. In Gissing's day he had time but little money and, after the first successful start, the lack of money ate into the time. Still, the little money Gissing had was his and he lived in a low-cost society. In our high-cost society we have money, but a large portion of it goes back to the State and we may not invest in our talent. In consequence, we have no time.

Morley Roberts, who was an intimate of Gissing, thought that he shared with most English novelists the ability to create situation and the inability to develop it owing to the national *mauvaise honte* and dread of feeling. But Gissing excelled, as many have, in irony. Each character is solid in *New Grub Street* and if the dialogue is still and the action is slow, there is nothing wooden in the people. Their temperature is, indeed, low. In their varying ways, they are all afflicted, of course, with Gissing's chronic passivity; but in two instances, in the characters of Reardon's wife Amy, and the young, climbing, versatile journalist, Jasper Milvain, he introduces us to two new and disturbing developments of the passive character. Milvain is not passive in his profession; he climbs boldly, cleverly, even engagingly; it is his conscience that is passive. He practises an ingenious technique of self-deception: *i.e.* he believes that if he is frank about his motives, if he tells the truth, this will clear him of moral obligations. He has the insincerity of the detached. Amy's passivity is feminine, and realistic. She has no will but she drifts with skill. Gissing is unusual among English male novelists in discerning the mental life of his women. Living in an ideal world himself he understood their ideal world. It did not shock him that Amy should resent her husband's failure; and that her love would not stand up to it. It was natural to wish to marry a great man, but it was also natural that, under his influence, she would develop into a creature alien to him and with an intellect of her own. She marries the conscienceless Milvain with her eyes open and with a delicate lack of scruple. Easy enough to make fun of her as a female climber; Gissing sees the comedy but he is detached enough to see she has a right to drift with her self-esteem. She will become genteel. Poverty is over.

When we wince at Gissing's uncritical acceptance of the lower-middle-class dream of gentility and respectability, and at its emblem, the butterfly collar; when we shudder at the tepid, timid ideal world he obtained from classical scholarship, we ought also to point out that he saw people in two troubled phases; as they are and as they would wish to become. To him the individual dream was or could become a serious extension of their emotional range as characters. Indeed, it is out of the soured homes, where dreams have gone bad, or have become ludicrous or catastrophic, that the vitality of this class has sprung. To most English novelists, invigorated but narrowed by class consciousness, one class has always seemed comical to another; that is where Gissing is so un-English, a foreigner or an exile. He sees nothing comic in class. He writes as if it exists chiefly as a pathos or a frustration, a limitation of the human keyboard.

MISS LONELYHEARTS

NATHANAEL WEST is one of the novelists of the breakdown of the American dream in the 'thirties. His real name was Nathan Weinstein, he moved in fashionable literary society, became a script writer in Hollywood after the success of *Miss Lonelyhearts* and was killed in a motor accident at the age of forty. Two of his novels, *Miss Lonelyhearts* —which is very well known—and *The Day of the Locust*, show that a very original talent was cut short. He was preoccupied with hysteria as the price paid for accepting the sentimentalities of the national dream. He feared hysteria in himself, he was morbidly conscious of it in his people; he was attracted and repelled by its false dreams as one might be by a more poisonous way of mixing gin. West did not feel that life was tragic, for the sense of tragedy was lost in the moral collapse of the period he lived in. Like Chekhov—but only in this respect—he was appalled by the banality of city civilisation. Instead of being tragic, life was terrible, meaningless and without dignity. Mr Alan Ross, in a warm, if sometimes difficult, introduction to a volume containing all four of West's novels, makes this point and suggests that while the English writers of the 'thirties reached their conclusions "through a series of well-bred intellectual convictions", Americans like West were thrown helplessly among the brute economic facts. For them the experience was emotional and even theatrically so, because hysterical violence is very near the surface in American life.

West's resources were Art—he learned from the surrealists—and compassion. Except in his satire, *A Cool Million*, which is an American *Candide* done in the manner of a parody too obvious and prolonged, he was not a political writer in the literal sense. He explored the illness behind the political situation. Human beings have always fought misery with dreams, Miss Lonelyhearts observes; the dream and its ignoble deceits, the panic, anger and frustration these deceits expose, gave him his material. In *The Day of the Locust*, his mature novel, it is the boredom exposed by the failure of the Californian dream of an earthly Paradise that puts an expression of hate and destructiveness on the faces of the weary middle-aged population who have retired to Los Angeles. As they pour in to gape at the stars arriving for some world première, they have the look of lynchers. Lynch, in fact, they do, and for no reason.

This does not convey that West is a comic writer. He has freakishness, wit and a taste for the absurd from the surrealists, also their sophistication in parody and styles, but moved quickly away from their gratuitous and perverse humour. He became comic and humane. *Miss Lonelyhearts* is a potent and orderly distillation of all the attitudes to human suffering. Miss Lonelyhearts himself is the drunken writer of an Advice Column in a newspaper who begins running it as a joke, a sort of sobbing *Americana*, and ends by becoming overwhelmed by the weight of human misery and by his inability to do anything about it. The office gambits sicken him. Christ, Art, the Karamazov line, the Value of Suffering, back to Nature, on to Hedonism and so on have been taped long ago by Shrike, the editor with the deadpan face, an expert in "how to play it". Shrike is one of West's many attacks on the dream-generators of the mass-media—an attack in the sense of being one of those unholy recognitions that lie at the centre of the comic view of life:

"I am a great saint," Shrike cried. "I can walk on my own water. Haven't you heard of Shrike's passion in the

> Luncheonette, or the Agony in the Soda Fountain? Then I compared the wounds in Christ's body to the mouths of a miraculous purse in which we deposit the small change of our sins. It is an excellent conceit. But now let us consider the holes in our own bodies and into what these congenital wounds open. Under the skin of a man is a wondrous jungle where veins like lush tropical growths hang along overripe organs and weed-like entrails writhe in squirming tangles of red and yellow. In this jungle, flitting from rock grey lungs to golden intestines, from liver to lights and back to liver again, lives a bird called the soul."

In the vulgar, exhausted way of the mass-media, deadpan Shrike is an aesthete. His jaunty little face looks like a paralysed scream of fright. His remarks are pictorial, but without relation to any meaning. Miss Lonelyhearts is muddled by Shrike's cleverness. He would like to be able to believe in the efficacy of Christ, but the name for him has become another word for hysteria, "a snake whose scales are tiny mirrors in which the dead world takes on a semblance of life". He plowters through a series of alcoholic bouts, tries to seduce Shrike's cold and salacious wife, gets into fights in speakeasies, terrorises and tries to torture an old man in a public lavatory; for Miss Lonelyhearts has strong sadistic fantasies, his pity has a strain of cruelty in it and he has begun to hate the sufferers who have the tempting horror of freaks. He is seduced by the nymphomaniac wife of a cripple, tries illness, love on a farm. These struggles are fuddled but heroic; he feels his "great heart" is a bomb that "will wreck the world without rocking it". In the end he has a vision of the love of Christ and rushes to tell his friend the cripple about it; but the cripple shoots him in a fit of jealousy. Christ may not be hysteria, but he is a tale told by an idiot.

This might have been a slushy book, the derelict lot behind James Barrie's hoardings. It is, instead, a selection of hard, diamond-fine miniatures, a true American fable. West writes very much by the eye and his use of poetic images has a precision which consciously sustains his preoccupation with the human being's infatuation with his dream and inner story. (All his people are spiders living in the webs they spin out of their minds.) Leaves on trees are like thousands of little shields, a woman's breasts are like "pink-tipped thumbs", a thrush sings like a "flute choked with saliva", a cripple limps along "making waste motions, like those of a partially destroyed insect". If we call *Miss Lonelyhearts* a minor star it is because we feel that the Art is stronger than the passion; that, indeed Miss Lonelyhearts himself is capable only of pathos. His advice to the nymphomaniac who is torturing her husband, to "let him win once", is just wise old owlishness; her happiness is to accuse and torture, his to drag his loaded foot. West has not considered that human beings overwhelmingly prefer suffering to happiness and that their sobbing letters are part of the sense of the role or drama that keeps them going. Still, as a performance, *Miss Lonelyhearts* is very nearly faultless.

The Day of the Locust is an advance from fable and from fragments of people, to the courageous full statement of the novel. I say "courageous" because in this kind of transition the writer has to risk showing the weakness of his hand. The artificial lights of the freak show are off in this book and we see human absurdity as something normal. This is a novel about Hollywood. West worked in the hum of the American dream generators and he chose those people who have done more for American culture than their coevals in Europe have done for theirs: the casualties, the wrecks, the failures, the seedy and the fakes. They are the people to whom the leisureless yea-sayers have said "No". The observer is a painter from the East who is dreaming up what sounds like a very bad picture, a sort of Belshazzar's Feast. (He is a vestige of West, the aesthete.) He has fallen for Faye, a day-dreaming creature who secretly earns money as a call-girl for a "cultured" brothel, and who hopes, like others in the novel, to get into pictures. She lives among a ramshackle group which includes old stage hangers-on, a ferocious dwarf, a woman who is grooming her son to be a wonder-child of the screen, an absurd, fairly genuine cowboy extra and a pathetic hotel clerk from the Middle West. Faye is carefully observed. She is the complete day-dreamer, insulated to such an extent by the faculty that it acts as an effective alternative to innocence; she is sexually provoking, cold, little-minded and cruel, but puts gaiety into the roles she takes on and has the survival power of a cork in a storm. If Los Angeles were destroyed by fire she would easily survive, not because she is hard but because she is flimsy. Already, in *Miss Lonelyhearts*, West had been a delicate student of the American bitch.

This Hollywood novel is mature because the compassion has no theatrical pressure; because now West is blocking in a sizeable society, and because his gift for inventing extraordinary scenes has expanded. The novel is dramatised—in Henry James's sense of the word—in every detail, so that each line adds a new glint to the action. His sadistic streak comes out in an astonishing description of an illegal cockfight in a desert lot. His comic powers fill out in the scenes with the angry dwarf and in the pages where the hero gets lost in a film Battle of Waterloo. The psychological entangling is brought to an appalling climax when Faye leaves her exhausted hotel clerk for a Mexican and this leads on to the great final staging of the world première, where riot and lynching are sparked off by the wonder boy of the screen and the hate behind the Californian myth comes out:

> Once there, they discover that sunshine is not enough. They get tired of oranges, even of avocado pears and passion fruit. Nothing happens. They haven't the mental

> equipment for leisure, the money nor the physical equipment for pleasure. . . . Their boredom becomes more and more terrible. They realise that they have been tricked and burn with resentment. Every day of their lives they read the newspapers and go to the movies. Both feed them on lynchings, murder, sex crimes, explosions, wrecks, love nests, fires, miracles, revolutions, war. This daily diet makes sophisticates of them. The sun is a joke. Oranges can't titillate their jaded palates. Nothing can be violent enough to make taut their slack minds and bodies.

It was a warning against Fascism; it makes the witch-hunt understandable; by extension, it is a statement about the nearness of violence in American life.

The Day of the Locust has the defect of insufficient ambition. It calls for a larger treatment and we have a slight suspicion that the painter-observer is slumming. But West had not the breath for full-length works. Script-writing snaps up the clever. His important contribution to the American novel was his polished comedy, which he displayed with the variety of a master and on many levels. If his talent was not sufficiently appreciated in the moral 'thirties, it was because comedy as a world in itself and as a firm rejection of the respected was not understood. West had something of Europe in him, where it is no crime to know too much.

HENRI DE MONTHERLANT

HENRI DE MONTHERLANT was born in 1896. He belongs to the brilliant generation of rebels on whom the label Recalcitrant and Unseizable can be fixed. "There have been three passions in my life: independence, indifference and physical delight", he has written; the words were sharpened in the trenches of the first World War to which we can trace his anti-romanticism and the determination to strip away the disguises of experience and to present only the "authentic". In *La Rose de Sable* (*Desert Love*) he wrote: "For we should all be most suspicious of any venture of spirit or conscience which we knew had begun by being merely one of the heart." His hostile studies of women, more particularly bourgeois women, in the pre-war novels, sprang from this mistrust of the duplicity of the heart: their speciality. Desire revitalises; love corrupts because it is corrupt in itself. In an interesting introduction Mr Quennell reminds us that the ruthless Montherlant hero used to be compared with Renaissance man. Well! Well! Nowadays he looks simply like one more writer; tough indeed, but evasively bent on self-preservation. In a long account of how he set out to make his life in his *Selected Essays*, he describes how he broke his ties with France after the first World War and went off to live anonymously and alone, in complete freedom in Algeria. He had ceased to be a Catholic; he was attracted to Spanish mysticism. Spanish critics found in him that intellectual excess which they always dislike in French culture when it seeks an exotic, foreign trellis. The essays are the work of a man of changeable and restless temper and the ones he wrote during the 'thirties when Hitler was rising, are egotistical and, on the whole, silly. Where he impressed, as Mr Quennell says, is as a descriptive writer. In this volume, Montherlant's account of his irritable, defensive acquaintanceship with a Jewish soldier during the first World War is worth the rest of the book. It is at once a portrait and an exact, cold estimate of his own prejudices as a stupid young man.

Since the second World War, Montherlant has emerged as a fine playwright. His novels seem less important. His attitude to life is interesting now only as it contributes to his descriptive power. Montherlant's descriptions are drained of personal excess and present a scene as if it were the residue left when dozens of conflicting eyes and minds have moved away from it. There is one novel which, because it lies outside his usual belligerence, begins to look like lasting. This is *The Bachelors* (*Les Célibataires*) published in 1934 and translated by Mr Terence Kilmartin. It is one of those carefully framed, precise and acid studies on a small canvas in which French writers again and again excel. The small becomes vast. Cosiness vanishes from cosy corners. Eccentricity is seen to be tragic. Two absurd old men cease to be only absurd; their comedy is dreadful. Their tale contains one of the repressed subjects of our time, one of the subjects that has in fact been secreted while our society has been devoting itself to "independence, indifference and physical delight", for Montherlant's three passions were not peculiar to him; they are principles that, by now, have taken possession of two generations. The subject is old age.

The two bachelors are an elderly uncle and his nephew, the survivors of a family of the Breton nobility who share a little house in filth and poverty in the Boulevard Arago. We meet the older one standing outside a lighted shop window reading a newspaper with the help of a stamp collector's magnifying glass. He looks like a tramp. His clothes date back to the fashions of 1885; his overcoat and all his clothes are fastened by safety pins, his boots are tied with string. His pockets contain an old crust of bread, two lumps of sugar, bits of tobacco, solid bread pellets and a beautiful gold watch with his coat of arms on it. He is Elie de Coëtquidan, a baron. At home, he sleeps in a filthy bed. He is hysterically devoted to cats. He is a keen remover of stamps from envelopes. He has fits of writing scandalous anonymous letters, for he delights in causing trouble. He is avaricious and dishonest. The only secret in his life is that he is a virgin; but since his principle is to frighten his other surviving relation, a richer banker, he pretends that a Jewish lady, to whom he takes a few sausages or cakes every Saturday, has been his mistress for thirty years or more and may make claims on the family. He is maliciously trading on the family's latent anti-semitism.

The nephew, Léon de Coantrés, goes about in workman's clothes. After a promising beginning—he excelled at Latin verse, played the piano, invented a photographic enlarger—he sank into neurotic sloth. His natural direction was downhill. He loathes Society and his ideal is to be an odd-job man or labourer, fetching coal, sweeping up, polishing floors—anything that requires no thought and no worry. He has by now cut himself off from women of his own class; in any case, his love affairs had been with servants and prostitutes; the sudden disappearance of one of these, for whom he had a tenderness had given him a powerful shock. For twenty-five years he has dreamed of her and never spoken to a woman. He washes once a fortnight. His whole life is based on a resentment of his aristocratic birth; and he suffers from the public scorn given to the French aristocracy. A clue to his neurotic condition is that his father had ruined the family and that he, the son, is being stripped, little by little, by newly discovered creditors of the family. With bewilderment he sees his tiny income vanishing. When the novel opens we see him trying to make his uncle face up to the terrible fact that they will have to sell up and separate. The loneliness of old age is about to set in.

And here the familiar French drama of avarice and hypocrisy begins. Uncle and nephew visit lawyers and their rich relative Octave, a banker—a beautifully drawn study in the evasions of a man who covers up his dishonesties by convincing himself of his own charitableness. He insures himself by openly deceiving himself. For example, when he realises that he is about to be touched by the old gentlemen, he at once gives a largish sum to an orphanage so that he will be able to say "in all honesty" that he has "so many claims". His other motive is that he is being sued by a tenant for charging an illegal rent, and the charity is a sop to his conscience. The gift is secret, yet in his idiotic way, he feels it will help his lawsuit morally!

Of the two supplicants, the malign elder is more successful. In a splendid scene he bluntly blackmails the banker with the totally unreal threat that he will go and live with his Jewish "mistress". He gets an allowance at once and then sits in the banker's splendid office and refuses to go, getting the utmost out of Octave's humiliation.

Being fundamentally innocent, Léon does worse. He is down to his last few francs and still the banker shuffles and evades. The household is broken up and then, suddenly, the baron reluctantly lets him live in the lodge of his summer château. The last evening of the two old men together is nearly wrecked by a small incident. The old one is rolling up a filthy bread pellet as he chatters and suddenly he stops and a wild look comes into his eyes.

> "What is it Uncle?" asked Léon anxiously.
>
> "I've lost my pellet," said the old man with a look of desperation. Léon got down on his hands and knees and searched with him. When he saw it, he hesitated; then he remembered that it was his last evening with his uncle and,

> in the name of the past, the family and his mother's memory, he picked up the ignoble object and gave it to him.

We come to the final scene where Léon goes enthusiastically to the little place of his own in the country. He will be "away from Society", in the "bosom of nature", "living the life of the common people". (Montherlant is mordant about class masochism.) He eats with the labourers at the inn who call him Monsieur le Comte for a day or two, but stop at once in terrible silence when he tells them he is poor. The minuteness of Montherlant's descriptions of a sick old man's empty days is terrible. One can count the hours. He can't think of anything to do, so he lies in bed; but once he is in bed, a log rolls off the fire or the chimney smokes and he has to get out. He begins to feel dizzy and ill.

> Like a drowning man searching desperately for something to cling on to, he wanted to concentrate on some action or other, so he snatched up a pair of nail clippers and cut his nails . . . He went to look at himself in the mirror, convinced that it must show in his face that he was a sick man. But he could see nothing abnormal in his face. He simply found it ludicrous.

Outside he can see the formations of wild geese flying away over the dunes in their autumn migration. The lines might come out of a Russian novel.

Montherlant's picture of old age is searing in its intimacy and the effect is all the more keen because he has a searching comic gift. The snobbish, negligent and dirty country doctor to whom Léon goes is a comic figure; and, back in the Paris pages, there is a brilliant short sketch of an aristocratic lady who finds Léon and pretends not to notice he is looking like a tramp, and shouts with ecstasy about his "simple life" and how "ravishing" it is. She would (Montherlant observes) have called *The Critique of Pure Reason* ravishing. Montherlant never skims the surface; he knows the habits of life, mind and speech of the different social classes, and especially of the aristocracy; and without labouring his points, can exactly place any word or act in its context. His sense of *milieu* is exact. His epigrams do not wear so well—it was clever in the 'thirties for a novelist to make a mocking intervention; it was a dig at literature. But his irony devastates. After Léon's death, the innkeeper sends to Octave the banker a heavy bill for drinks the wretched Léon has never had; and Octave pays up willingly. He can now quieten his own conscience with the happy delusion that Léon's total failure as a human being was due to alcohol. The key to Montherlant's outlook on life is contained in an armed sentence: "People do not do us all the harm they are capable of." One lives in danger, on the edge of things. Montherlant's distinction is that he writes a prose that catches perfectly this sense that the course of life is perilous and unexpected.

Algeria, the romantic and patriotic cult of the Sahara: Montherlant's *Desert Love* is a novelist's response to "the colonial situation" and the private dilemma of the conqueror. The introduction to the English translation by Alec Brown, is not clear about this book. It has been drastically cut. The translation is from the French edition of 1955 and this is an extract from a much longer manuscript written in 1932. I am not sure whether this has ever been published; the suppressed portion is political. Why suppressed? Out of date, perhaps; or the author has changed his mind. We ought to be told and we are not. The book is evidently an attack on the conventional, upper-class European, nature's Second-in-Command. His class has dulled him. The present story contains the love story only of the original manuscript, and this is complete in itself. Love is M. de Montherlant's speciality: women are pitiable or contemptible instruments, men are exasperated executants. The curse upon man is the worship of maturity. Love is regarded as a delusive transaction between technicians who have engaged in it out of *amour propre* and are surprised by emptiness, hypocrisy, suffering and loneliness. Passivity predominates in his characters; from this they go on to cruelty and pity. They are hurt and hurting. Aiming at exactitude (which is not possible without heart) Montherlant's view is fundamentally perverse, but it has edge and clarity. He lacks the faculty and humility of human blindness.

Desert Love is one more of his examinations of the insulted and the injured. By the influence of his patriotic and socially influential mother, Lieutenant Auligny is posted to a remote station in the Sahara. She wants the glamour of a son "out there". He, too, is willing to believe in it. Lacking intellect, he is a passive passenger of contemporary rhetoric. He is ready to believe in the Sahara myth and when this illusion is quickly killed he falls back on the grumpy chauvinism of small things. This is good: upper-class chauvinism has become petty. Auligny is good, upright, kind, without military ambition and stupid. He is also morbidly sensitive. If we compare him with his English opposite number, the nice or decent fellow, Auligny probably lacks the group or social instinct which is second nature to the English and is their conventional hide-out when in personal difficulties. Auligny tries to think consistently; his opposite number would grope his way through an undergrowth of sentiment and worry. Auligny finds that the Sahara post is hell on earth. Heat, squalor, boredom, have driven the older hands to near-madness, drink and squalid nights with the one local prostitute. Auligny decides that he can keep his sanity if he finds an Arab girl companion. There must be some human tenderness which will give him security of spirit. A girl is quite easily contracted for; she is hardly more than an inarticulate, illiterate and obedient child. It upsets Auligny that he has had to rent her; it fusses him that the contract requires that she shall remain virgin—a conflict here between honour and personal vanity.

Auligny is a man without self-confidence. He invites a friend (the familiar artist-Casanova of French fiction whom one never really believes in) to share the girl. Guiscart-Casanova foresees the worst; a connoisseur of bizarre sexual situations, he refuses at the last minute. The effect on Auligny is excessive. The girl yields to him suddenly and he is in love with her. He is not only mentally entangled now; he becomes pro-Arab.

> Nobody even suspects the business of carnal love at the root of this or that action of ours which today seems so disinterested. And presumably this is all to the good. For we should all be most suspicious of any venture of spirit or conscience which we knew had begun by being merely one of the heart.

The last sentence there is more interesting than the first: as a minor La Rochefoucauld, Montherlant is apt to fire only on one cylinder.

A parallel sympathy for the French is not, as we can see, aroused in the sandy, illiterate and passive girl. Goodness knows—Montherlant doesn't—what sex does for her. She is well-drawn and is certainly not sentimentalised. Once awakened she quickly tires; in any case, Auligny is a man who watches. He does not give. Neither she nor her father sees in him anything but the conqueror who commands and pays. Their desperate hunger is not sexual. The soft-hearted Auligny wishes to get more out of sex alone than can be bought, or is even there to buy. He is rejected. She and the one or two Arabs are silent when he makes pro-Arab remarks—a characteristic situation of the 'thirties.

They do not hate him. They find him laughable. The reason seems to be that they are secure through living with their race; he is insecure, like a child whose pride is to pretend to be alone. There is the passing gaiety of the flesh. What else is there? (Auligny asks.) He calls the girl "the sand rose" because "she resembled those little petrifications in being as charming as their petals on the surface, but underneath as cold and inert as the stone of which they are formed".

Montherlant is a tender and exact analyst of the pagan processes of lust and his descriptions of carnal love are intimate without coarseness. He is not one of those erotic novelists who describe in order to excite themselves. Even in a brutal or squalid scene he keeps his head. His success here springs from the fact that he is more interested in the mind as the body affects it. His chief curiosity is for the character of Auligny, in pulling to pieces a character who combines stupidity and sensibility. Above all Montherlant is interested in the worry and pathos of human inconsistency. In "the colonial situation", indeed in any human situation, there is no such thing as a fixed type. Montherlant's other novels have left an impression of emotional immaturity, but this works to his advantage in describing the abortive love of transaction. And if there is something intrinsically mean in the scale and people of the episode, his strong physical feeling for the desert gives a larger impression of loneliness, desuetude and the grinding-down of life:

> For he was now wide awake, in the centre of the bivouac, drowned in the pungency of the troop's leather, and staring into starless sky. With strident whinnies, just like so many women laughing, some of the horses struggled and stamped their hooves, trying to get free from their hobbles. A man went across to tighten the knots. At last there was quiet. Auligny rolled over on the other side. Under the ash, the fire seemed to be out, but every now and then a little flame leapt up to illuminate the *shesh*-enwrapped head of one of the men, a shadowy bundle on

the ground. . . . All around him his men lay asleep, their faces completely covered or with the *shesh* concealing their mouths. They sprawled like children, some so covered and bundled up that one would not have suspected they were human beings at all, others the opposite stretched out in the naivest postures. Some forearms were stretched up stiff in the air. There were lovely rings on the fingers of some of the uncouth soldiers. Their knuckles gleamed.

Were they human, was the Berber girl human? The conqueror's mind was tortured. He had the vanity of his principles, the burden of his backslidings. The sandstorm reduced one to frantic animal restlessness. It blew up the stench of smoke, turned the air to glue and rustled maddeningly on the dunes. In the heat one could have been lying under the furnace of a locomotive. A knife could have been stuck fast in the dense air. They told Auligny to keep cool by singing: "Lah, lah, lah, lah."

The portrait of Auligny is dispassionate and exhaustive. He is the well-brought-up young man, uprooted and lost. His difficulty is his inadequacy for the role of conqueror; very few can naturally fill it—those who know and those who do not ask. Auligny even lacks the desire for military distinction. His sensibility is really self-regarding and, when out of his depth, he is either brutal or wounded. His "case"—if he has one—is that he has never really moved out of Paris and in any very serious novel about the colonial situation, he is really not strong enough to be fully in it. He never really finds out about the Arabs, indeed in his humiliation, he cries out against the High Command for sending inexperienced men who do not know the language to the country. He is taken aback when he observes a "human" reaction in the Arabs—if he sees tears or some "unreasonable" behaviour. He is crushed when the girl he has bought does not love him and tells lies.

What has all this to do with Algeria? Isn't it a good deal

just the dear old French theme of the bought little mistress, something neat about the disappointments of too-neat an idea? It is not Montherlant's fault that the Auligny situation is now out of date. He has done what he set out to do—to reduce the exotic Sahara myth to the experience of one of its nonentities. Implicit in this is also the exposure of nonentity love: the love that fears to meet an equal. In its erotic pages French literature has colonised wildly since the Romantic movement. That is now put right. Auligny rides off with his dream in his head, like any other sad officer in French fiction, but "trampled underfoot". It is "a closed dream". The road back is barred by ridicule. He has not even the consolation of remorse. It is as if the young ladies in Chekhov had had no intention ever of going to Moscow. There is not even Good-bye. End of the European myth of the departing garrison.

THE TIN-OPENERS

ONE of the nice things about foreigners is their faithful regard for English light humour. When we disclaim it, when we snobbishly indicate that this fanciful persiflage goes out of date very quickly, they reproach us. If we explain that the speciality had become sententious at the turn of the century and was in decline after 1914, when wit, impatience, cruelty and vivid scorn returned to our comic writing, the foreign reader persists that our gracious light humour was civilisation itself. Victorian civilisation, we may reply; but millions have read a book like Jerome K. Jerome's *Three Men in a Boat*, and in all the languages of Europe and Asia. One would hardly have thought that this modest little tale of the misadventures of three tin-opening suburban clerks on the Thames would stand up to American connoisseurs of Mark Twain's Mississippi, but it did. Pirated at once, the book conquered America as it amused the students of Bombay, Peking and Valparaiso.

The gag-book, of course, follows the flag. It is now American. The American response to Jerome arose possibly because he had the episodic, digressing, garrulous quality of their vernacular writers. He is close to the Twain of *The Jumping Frog*. But Jerome, like the authors of *The Diary of a Nobody*, and like W. W. Jacobs, belongs to a secure, small Arcadia where the comic disasters of life are the neater for being low. Jerome's humour is a response of the emerging lower middle class to the inconvenience of their situation. Their dreams have left a legacy of small comic defeat. Overworked, they regard idleness as a joke. They have to do everything in penn'orths and ha'porths. Genteel, they have to repress their hilarious envy-disapproval of any burst of bad language on the part of the undeserving poor. The humour of life's little troubles was called the "too real", the joke lying in deadly and misleading accounts of humiliating trivia. One might take Jerome as the signal that, in 1889, holidays for this overworked and masochistic class became possible. It is "too real" that the tin-opener (new emancipating gadget of democracy) has been forgotten. It is "too real" that George and Harris have to share the same bed; that the bed is two foot six wide and that they have to tie themselves together with the sheets in order to keep themselves from falling out. It is "too real", *i.e.*, only too likely, that the dog will bring a rat to drop into the terrible stew they are making. It is "too real" that a worn-out child will drop a half-eaten bun in the maze at Hampton Court. The packing, the rain, the clubbing together to hire a cab, the mockery of small boys, the troubles with towropes, laundry, butter, the belief that the banjo is a lovely instrument and that *Two Lovely Black Eyes* is a beautiful song are the vulgarities of life. There is nothing surreal about the "too real"; it is the chronic. We know little about the inner lives of Jerome's characters. It is true that Harris has a comic nightmare, but this is merely the traditional joke about strong drink. The odd thing is that the "too real" could be appreciated in Bombay. Is the tale of Uncle Podger a universal domestic myth? Would Arabs laugh at it? The appeal of Jerome lies in his gentleness and irony, in his power of digression, his gift of capping his comic moments with a final extravagant act that outbids life altogether. Above all, his book is an idyll. Jerome himself, astonished by the book's success, guilefully argued that it could not be due to its vulgarity alone. The absence of women gives us a clue—there is one, but she is a mere body that floats by, drowned: *Three Men in a Boat* has the absurdity of a male pipe dream. *Huckleberry Finn* is basically this also; but the tobacco is stronger and indeed, generally, chewed.

The idyll is the stream on which the vulgar, bickering, banjo-playing boat-load floats lightly along. Not lightly, of course; sculling blisters and half kills them. The joke lies in the modesty of the incident; bumping the bank, getting someone else's shirt wet, eating the horrible camping food, annoying fishermen and motor launches, singing with self-confidence and out of tune, drifting unawares towards the weir, getting the tent up for the night. A lot of it is stock comedy. We know the tent will fall down; the question that awakens the ingenuity of the masters is, how will it fall down? At Cookham these suburbans will imagine themselves in the "wild heart of nature". They are not mugs; they have to match their bounce against the primeval cunning of landladies and the pensive malice of innkeepers, anglers and boatmen. Skilfully Jerome plays everything down. He relies on misleading moral commentary and on that understatement which runs like a rheumatism through English humour. Certain jokes date. Bad language is no longer a joke since swearing came in after the first World War. Idleness is no longer a joke—we have moved into an age that says it believes in leisure. And we find nothing piquant in the silliness of girls. The silly girl in light humour was soon replaced by Wodehouse's pretty power stations. (The light humorists of Jerome's period were obliged to avoid sex; they became experts in femininity.) But the dating of a joke does not matter; the laughter in Jerome is caused less by any fact than by the false conclusions drawn from it. He will mildly note that bargees are sometimes "rude" to one another and use language "which, no doubt, in their calmer moments, they regret". Again the work-joke has the intricacy of a conceit in Jerome's skilful hands.

> It always seems to me that I am doing much more work than I should do. . . . But though I crave for work I still

> like to be fair. I do not ask for more than my fair share. But I get it without asking for it—so at least it seems to me and this worries me. George says that he does not think that I need trouble myself on the subject. He thinks it is only my over-scrupulous nature that makes me fear I am having more than my due; and that, as a matter of fact, I don't have as much as I ought. But I expect he says this only to comfort me.

The son of a preacher, Jerome saw that one of the funniest things about a human being is his conscience.

The light humorists get too much pleasure out of educated periphrasis and self-congratulatory club wit. These lead inevitably to heavy prose. Jerome, like W. W. Jacobs, escaped the danger. His prose is clear and simple. It muses on like some quiet, ironical tune played on a malicious whistle. He is free from the journalistic vice of exhibitionism and frantic juggling with bright ideas. He sits by himself on the river bank and drifts on from tune to tune, happily and regardless. He is a very economical writer. In anecdote, he is a master of leading the reader on quietly and then of rushing in a line that suddenly makes the joke take to the air and go mad. The tale of Uncle Podger hanging the picture is a notable piece of technical virtuosity. The packing of the trunk begins as a joke but ends in the complexity of French farce or Restoration comedy. The good light humorist is not a careless fellow with one or two brainwaves and surprises only; he is a deedy lover of the detail that delays the action until the pressure has reached the proper bursting point. There are some conventional phrases in Jerome's famous account of opening the tin of pineapple, but it is a model. They had tried the penknife, a pair of scissors and a hitcher: the tin merely rolled over, broke a tea cup and fell into the river. George and Harris were no more than a little cut about the face:

> Then we all got mad. We took that tin out on the bank and Harris went up into a field and got a big sharp stone and I went back into the boat and brought out the mast, and George held the tin and Harris held the sharp end of his stone against the top of it and I took the mast and poised it high in the air and gathered all my strength and brought it down.
>
> It was George's straw hat that saved his life that day . . . Harris got off with a flesh wound.
>
> After that I took the tin off myself and hammered at it with the mast till I was worn out and sick at heart whereupon Harris took it in hand.
>
> We beat it out flat; we beat it back square; we battered it into every form known to geometry. Then George went at it and knocked it into a shape so strange, so weird, so unearthly in its wild hideousness that he got frightened and threw away the mast. Then we all three sat down on the grass and looked at it.
>
> There was one great dent across the top that had the appearance of a mocking grin, and it drove us furious, so that Harris rushed at the thing and caught it up and flung it into the middle of the river, and as it sank we hurled our curses at it and we got into the boat and rowed away from the spot and never paused until we reached Maidenhead.

This is pure music hall, of course; much of Jerome is quiet comic patter. He was, in fact, something of an actor. But the idyll frames it all. And peacefully transforms it. A collection of light articles becomes a complete mirage. A world is never created on any level, without the secret structure of conflict. Jerome's case was like that of Dickens in the *Pickwick Papers*. He was commissioned to write an historical guide to the Thames and bits of that survive in the book. He was also a meditative man with a religious background. One or two little sermons are embedded in the text. To us they are incongruous, but late-Victorian farce was not hostile to sentiment. These pieties give an engaging wash of pure sentimental purple to

Jerome's water colour. He was always saved by his lightness of touch. He succeeds less with history. Jokes about Queen Elizabeth and Magna Carta are heavy going. It takes a schoolmaster or a Mark Twain to get the best out of them. Nonconformists like Jerome are apt to be too fervently conventional about history. As for the landscape, it is agreeably kept in its place. The glitter of the main stream, the rankness of the shadows, the gushing of the locks and the streaming of the weirs at night are done with a pleasant subdued versifying. These sights do not overwhelm his true business—that row of elderly anglers (for example) sitting on their chairs in a punt, who are suddenly knocked off, fall into the bottom of the boat and are left—in sublime phrase—"picking fish off each other".

Mr D. C. Browning, who writes an introduction to the Everyman Edition of the book, which contains also *Three Men on the Bummel*, tries to persuade us that the latter is as good. What the German tour does is to point to the reason for the superiority of the book about the Thames. It is an idyll of youth. In the German book the heroes are older. They are married. They have lost the happy, impartial rudeness of unattached young men. This time they have to be informative. They still sparkle, but the lark has turned into a tour. Jerome was very shrewd about the Germans and these, sedulously trying to penetrate the mystery of English fancy, used *Three Men on the Bummel* as a textbook in German schools.

THE BRUTAL CHIVALRY

ROBERT SURTEES is a sport, in both senses of the term, who flashes in and out of the English novel, excites hope and reduces the critical factions to silence. He has all the dash, all the partiality and all the prospect of an amateur. There is a rush of air, a shower of rain drops from the branches, a burst of thundering mud, a crashing of hazel, the sight of a pink coat and, as far as the English novel is concerned, he has gone. In that brief appearance he has made the genial suggestion that all the other English novelists have been mistaken; they have missed the basic fact in English life—that we are religious, that our religion is violent sport. The unwritten life of a large proportion of the characters in English fiction is passed in playing or watching games in the open air; nature is being worshipped with the senses and the muscles. We are either bemused by fresh air or are day-dreaming of some lazy, cunning and exhausting animal life in the open. In that condition, our hourly and sedentary habit of worry as a substitute for thought vanishes and we become people in love. It takes an amateur, like Surtees, to see an obvious thing like this and to exaggerate so that the part becomes the whole of English life. He was a north-country squire, an excellent sporting journalist, but handsomely innocent of the future of hunting in England. He really thought that the Industrial Revolution would make the sport democratic. His assumption is that English violence can be appeased only by the horse. He is the final authority on our horse civilisation, and Jorrocks is a sort of Don Quixote of the last phase of a brutal chivalry. *Après moi* (he might have said) *le garage.*

It is natural that hunting people should admire Surtees. It is not surprising that serious literary critics should admire him also. He creates a complete world. It is the world which Fielding's and Thackeray's people knew in their off-stage lives. It has no relation with the feeble sub-culture of horse-lovers, pony-worshippers, or with the gentility of the jodhpur that spread over England as the coach gave way to the railway, provoking the cult of the New Forest pony. The natural democrats of England live in the north and, though Surtees was a Tory squire, he sincerely believed that the horse was an insurance against the new, snobbish exclusiveness of the shot-up Victorian middle class. He imagined, as so many have done before, that class revolutions will not become snobbish and exclusive. Happy pastoral delusion! Surtees did not foresee either the hardness or the sentimentality of the coming urban England. Or, perhaps, he half guessed it. For the point about Jorrocks is that he is (1) not a horse-lover but a fox-lover, (2) that he rides, buys and sells horses, (3) that he has not an aitch to his name. He is, boldly, incontrovertibly, aggressively, in mid-nineteenth century—a grocer. His fame is that he is not merely a sportsman, but a Cockney sportsman. He has all the trading sharpness and romanticism of a man who sells tea. Surtees is content (purposefully content) with this reality. Jorrocks is as vulgar as Keats; and, as a northerner and a gentleman, Surtees refuses to accept the improved accents of the new-rich in the south. He exploits the rewards our class system offers to our literature. We are continually supplying a number of vulgar geniuses who stand out against the new snobberies which the Puritan streak in us is liable to create; and, in the case of Surtees, there is the anomaly that a Tory squire provides the vulgar protest. The heir of Jorrocks is Mr Polly. Both are native protests against the mean and successful revolutions that deny the instincts of genial, sincere and natural men.

Surtees owes a lot to the low side of Thackeray and does seamy society a good deal better. His dialogue is as quick and true as the master's. He extends a robust and native tradition: the masculine strain of English comic writing. This comedy is broad and extroverted. It grins at the pleasures and pains of the human animal—if it is male—and has little time for the female. Occasionally Surtees sees a tolerable female, but very rarely. We need not suppose that he agreed with Jorrocks that a man ought to kick his wife out of bed three times a month, but we suspect this was only because he regarded the act wistfully as an ideal unfortunately unattainable. The fact is that our comic extroverts are like Mr Sponge and bring a horse-dealer's eye to the consideration of women—"fifteen two and a half is plenty of height" for them. In its male world, the comic tradition likes the misfortunes of the body, the bruises, the black eyes, the drinking sessions, the gorging at table; prefers the low to the refined, the masterful and unreasonable to the sensitive and considerate. There is a strong regard for the impossible element in human character, for the eccentric and the obsessed. The brutes have their engaging moments. (They give the right kind of girl half a dozen smacking kisses.) But their transcendent emotions emerge in another direction. Jorrocks will quarrel with his huntsman, Pigg, but be reconciled, to the point of embracing him, at the kill. These people are dedicated. They will suffer anything, from drowning upwards, for their sport. They will experience an ecstasy which goes beyond the animal into the poetic. And, in the meantime, they will rollick. Thoroughly non-Puritan, they understand that the life of animal pleasure is the life of animal dismay and they accept it. What these writers in the masculine comic tradition dwell on is the variety of human character. They know that action brings this out, and with a kind of mercy, they will forgive anything so long as action, not introspection, has revealed it.

Mr Aubrey Noakes has written a good brief appreciation of Surtees*. It does not add to earlier studies, but it does bring out the importance of his experience with the law and his adventures in politics. Mr Noakes also goes into the interesting reluctance of the Victorians to take to him until Leech illustrated his novels. On the one hand, Surtees was a man of the eighteenth century—hence Thackeray's understanding of him; on the other, he was an amateur who dealt almost entirely with background figures, the great Jorrocks excepted. He was deeply knowing about English sporting life, the squirearchy and the law, but he did not construct the melodramas and elaborate plots of the other Victorian novelists, nor did he issue their moralisings. He often excelled them in the recording of ordinary speech and day-to-day incident. He is fresher than the masters, but he is artless. A good deal of his humour is the humour of shrewd sayings which, later on, we find in Kipling. His original contribution is in the field of invective. Surtees has a truly Elizabethan power of denunciation. Here is Jorrocks loosing off to his servant:

> "Come hup, you snivellin', drivellin' son of a lucifer-match maker," he roars out to Ben who is coming lagging along in his master's wake. "Come on," roars he, waving his arm frantically, as, on reaching Ravenswing Scar, he sees the hounds swinging down, like a bundle of clock pendulums into the valley below. "Come hup, I say, ye miserable, road-ridin', dish-lickin' cub! And give me that quad, for you're a disgrace to a saddle, and only fit to toast muffins for a young ladies' boarding school. Come hup, you preter-pluperfect tense of 'umbugs. . . . Come on, ye miserable, useless son of a lily-livered besom-maker. Rot ye, I'll bind ye 'prentice to a salmon-pickler."

This is all the more splendid because Jorrocks keeps to the "'ard road" as much as possible, and can't bear taking a fence.

* *Horses, Hounds and Humans*, Oldbourne Press, 1957.

He is eloquent, perhaps because he is as cowardly as Falstaff and yet as sincere in his passion. He knows what he wants to be. His is the eloquence of romance. And this is where we come to the Dickensian aspect of Surtees, too. Dickens has several degrees of comic observation. There is the rudimentary Dickens of caricature, of the single trait or phrase turned into the whole man. And there is the Dickens where this is elaborated into soliloquy, in which the character is represented by his fantasy life. Like the rudimentary Dickens, Surtees has the feeling for caricature. *Handley Cross*, *Facey Romford's Hounds* and *Mr Sponge's Tours* are packed with minor eccentrics of the field, the fancy and the law; but in Jorrocks, Surtees enters upon the more complex study of people who live out the comic orgy. "By 'eavens, it's sublime," says Jorrocks, watching the hounds stream over a hundred acres of pasture below him. "'Ow they go, screechin' and towlin' along just like a pocketful o' marbles . . . 'Ow I wish I was a heagle." A "heagle" he is, in that moment; sublimity is his condition. He has shrewdly built up his pack, he has given his uproarious lectures, he has had his vulgar adventures in country-houses; he has got the better of his betters and has outdone the new rich in vulgarity—making among other things that immortal remark about mince: "I like to chew my own meat"—he has disgraced Mrs Jorrocks, but he has pursued an obsession utterly, so that it has no more to teach him, beyond the fact that it has damaged his credit among the unimaginative in the City. Fortunately, Surtees has given him power of speech. Jorrocks is never at a loss for repartee or for metaphor. He is remarkable in his duels with Pigg, and the only pity is that Pigg's dialect is nearly incomprehensible. But Pigg and his master are well-matched. They battle like theologians about the true business of life: the pursuit of foxes.

Surtees is a specialist. But he is, to an important extent, outside his speciality. He had strong views about sport. He hated the drunkenness of sporting society and the old squirearchy. He hoped the new age would bring in something better. He was hostile to the literary conventions. His parodies of *Nimrod* show him as an opponent of literary snobbery. He disliked the obsequious regime of servants and the rogueries of the stable, the auctions and the law. It is odd that one so saturated in his world should have seen it all with so fresh an eye. Perhaps he had that morbidity of eye which is given to some men at the end of a period, when they can see things with the detachment which considerable art demands. He was too much the gentleman and amateur to construct a great novel; but he was independent enough and sufficiently instructed by obsession to create in Jorrocks a huge character who could go off and live an episodic life of his own. The Victorians were shy of Surtees's honesty. They were moving away from the notion that there was a level on which all Englishmen could be united. They were building the split-culture of our time. Surtees was trying to save England on the acres of Handley Cross.

THE PERFORMING LYNX

"I'M living so far beyond my income," says one of the characters in Saki's *The Unbearable Bassington*, "that we may almost be said to be living apart." That is a pointer to Saki's case: it is the fate of wits to live beyond the means of their feeling. They live by dislocation and extravagance. They talk and tire in the hard light of brilliance and are left frightened and alone among the empty wine-glasses and tumbled napkins of the wrecked dinner-table. Saki was more than a wit. There was silence in him as well. In that silence one sees a freak of the travelling show of story-tellers, perhaps a gifted performing animal, and it is wild. God knows what terrors and cajoleries have gone on behind the scenes to produce this gifted lynx so contemptuously consenting to be half-human. But one sees the hankering after one last ferocious act in the cause of a nature abused. The peculiar character called Keriway who crops up unexplained in the middle of the Bassington novel tells the story of a "tame, crippled crane". "It was lame," Keriway says, "that is why it was tame."

What lamed and what tamed Saki? The hate, passion, loneliness that closed the hearts of the children of the Empire-builders? Like Thackeray, Kipling and Orwell, Saki was one of the children sent "home" from India and Burma to what seemed to them loveless care. Saki did not suffer as Kipling suffered, but we hear of an aunt whom his sister described as a woman of "ungovernable temper, of fierce likes and dislikes, imperious, a moral coward, possessing no brains worth speaking of and a primitive disposition". A Baroness Turgenev, in short. She is thought to be the detested woman in *Sredni*

Vashtar, one of Saki's handful of masterpieces, the tale of the boy who plotted and prayed that she should be killed by a ferret. Boy and ferret were satisfied. But something less pat and fashionably morbid than a cruel aunt at Barnstaple must lie behind Saki's peculiarity, though she may go some way to explain his understanding of children. We are made by forces much older than ourselves. Saki was a Highland Scot and of a race that was wild and gay in its tribal angers. Laughter sharpens the steel. He belonged—and this is more important—to an order more spirited, melancholy, debonair and wanton than the puddingy Anglo-Saxon world south of the Border, with its middle-class wealth, its worry and its conventions. He could not resist joining it, but he joined to annoy. *The Unbearable Bassington* is a neat piece of taxidermy, a cheerful exposure of the glass case and contents of Edwardian society, a footnote to *The Spoils of Poynton*. In a way, Saki has been tamed by this society, too. Clovis likes the cork-pop of an easy epigram, the schoolboy hilarity of the practical joke and the fizz of instant success—"The art of public life consists to a great extent of knowing exactly where to stop and going a bit further" and so on—he is the slave of the teacup and dates with every new word. His is the pathos of the bubble. But Saki has strong resources: he is moved by the inescapable nature of the weariness and emptiness of the socialite life, though unable to catch, like Firbank, the minor poetry of fashion. Francesca is too shallow to know tragedy, but she will know the misery of not being able to forget what she did to her son, all her life. She is going to be quietly more humiliated every year. And then, Saki's other resource is to let the animals in with impudent cruelty. The leopard eats the goat in the Bishop's bathroom, the cat rips a house-party to pieces, the hounds find not a fox but a hyena and it comfortably eats a child; the two trapped enemies in the Carpathian forest make up their feud and prepare to astonish their rescuers with the godly news but the rescuers are wolves. Irony and polish are meant to lull us into amused, false comfort. Saki writes like an enemy. Society has bored him to the point of murder. Our laughter is only a note or two short of a scream of fear.

Saki belongs to the early period of the sadistic revival in English comic and satirical writing—the movement suggested by Stevenson, Wilde, Beerbohm, Firbank and Evelyn Waugh —the early period when the chief target was the cult of convention. Among these he is the teaser of hostesses, the shocker of dowagers, the mocker of female crises, the man in the incredible waistcoat who throws a spanner into the teacup; but irreverence and impudence ought not to be cultivated. They should occur. Otherwise writers are on the slippery slope of the light article. Saki is on it too often. There is the puzzling, half-redeeming touch of the amateur about him, that recalls Maurice Baring's remark that he made the mistake of thinking life more important than art. But the awkwardness, the jumpiness in some of these sketches, the disproportion between discursion and incident or clever idea has something to do with the journalism of the period—Mr Evelyn Waugh's suggestion—and, I would add, some connection with the decadence of club culture. The great period of that culture was in the mid-nineteenth century: by the early 1900's it had run into the taste for the thin, the urbane and the facetious; and to sententious clichés: Lady Bastable is "wont to retire in state to the morning-room"; Clovis makes a "belated appearance at the breakfast-table"; people "fare no better" and are "singularly" this or that. The cinema, if nothing else, has burned this educated shrubbery out of our comic prose. But Saki's club prose changes when he is writing descriptions of nature (in which he is a minor master) when he describes animals and children or draws his sharp new portraits. His people are chiefly the stupid from the county, the natterers of the drawing-room and the classical English bores, and though they are done in cyanide, the deed is touched by a child's sympathy for the vulnerable areas of the large mammals. He collected especially the petty foibles and practical vanities of women (unperturbed by sexual disturbance on his part), and so presented them as persons, just as he presented cats as cats and dogs as dogs.

> Eleanor hated boys and she would have liked to have whipped this one long and often. It was perhaps the yearning of a woman who had no children of her own.

Or there is the scene between the pleasant Elaine who, having just become engaged to be married, decides to increase her pleasure by scoring off her aunt and her country cousin who has also just got engaged. Saki is clear that Elaine is a thoroughly nice girl:

> "There is as much difference between a horseman and a horsy man as there is between a well-dressed man and a dressy one," said Elaine judicially, "and you have noticed how seldom a dressy woman really knows how to dress. An old lady of my acquaintance observed the other day, some people are born with a sense of how to clothe themselves, others acquire it, others look as if their clothes had been thrust upon them."

A stale joke? Beware of Saki's claws; he goes on in the next sentence:

> She gave Lady Caroline her due quotation marks, but the sudden tactfulness with which she looked away from her cousin's frock was entirely her own idea.

Saki's male bores and male gossips are remarkable in our comic literature, for he does not take the usual English escape of presenting them as eccentrics. Bores are bores, classifiable, enjoyable like anacondas or the lung-fish. There is Henry Creech with "the prominent, penetrating eyes of a man who can do no listening in the ordinary way and whose eyes have to perform the function of listening for him". And bores have lives. When Stringham made a witty remark for the first time in his life in the House of Commons one evening, remarking indeed that, "the people of Crete unfortunately make more history than they can consume locally", his wife grasped that some clever woman had got hold of him and took poison.

E. V. Knox's edition of Saki's tales (published by Collins) is a pleasant one, but it inexplicably omits all the stories from *Beasts and Superbeasts* in which Saki was at his best. I do not much care for Saki's supernatural stories, though I like the supernatural touch: the dog, for example, in *The Unbearable Bassington*, at the ghastly last dinner-party. His best things are always ingenious: the drama of incurring another's fate in *The Hounds of Fate*, the shattering absurdity of *Louis*, the artificial dog; and the hilarious tale of the tattooed Dutch commercial traveller who is confined to Italy because he is officially an unexportable work of art. The joke, for Saki, is in the kill. On the whole, it is the heart that is aimed at. He is always richly informed in the vanities of political life and does it in a manner that recalls Disraeli. Except for novels by Belloc, there has been none of this political writing since. Artificial writers of his kind depend, of course, on the dangerous trick-logic of contrivance. Success here is a gamble. For morality he substitutes the child's logic of instinct and idea.

The Unbearable Bassington is one of the lasting trifles. Its very surprising quality is the delicate apprehension of pleasure and misery. Saki was short of pity. He was an egotist and had no soothing word for pain. He knew that certain kinds of pain cannot be forgotten. Self-dramatisation, self-pity, none of the usual drugs, can take that stone from the heart. He is thoughtful but will offer nothing. In this frivolous novel Saki begins to mature. His next novel, *The Coming of William*, written in 1912 and warning lazy and corrupt Society of the German menace, was good propaganda. He imagined an England annexed to Germany and it makes uncomfortable reading; for silly Society turns instantly to collaboration. There is a more serious discomfort here; a disagreeable anti-Semitism shows more plainly in this book and one detects, in this soldierly sado-masochist, a desire for the "discipline" of authoritarian punishment. He is festive and enjoyable as the wild scourge; but the danger obviously was that this performing lynx, in the demi-monde between journalism and a minor art, might have turned serious and started lecturing and reforming his trainer. In earlier and more spontaneous days, he would have eaten him.

HUGO'S IMPERSONATIONS

"HUGO began life as a mature man and is only now entering on adolescence." The words of Vigny's referred to Hugo's life when he was twenty-seven, not to his work, but they come back when we read *Notre-Dame de Paris* and *Les Misérables.* There are dreams we dream no longer, powerful frescoes without intimacy. They belong to the volcanic periods of life—so apt to return—when the unconscious erupts, when the super-ego pronounces, when the monstrous and the ideal hog or transfigure our natures, when the self is still molten and has not been hardened into unproductive habit. In Hugo, it never became hardened. He spread into journalism and epic. Content to impersonate medieval history in *Notre-Dame de Paris*, Hugo became universal history, man, justice, natural and spiritual law, the Infinite by the time he came to the 2900 pages of *Les Misérables.* It has been said that, like Balzac, he had too much confidence in his own genius. So had all the Romantics. The criticism is useless: take away excess from Hugo and the genius vanishes. One has to agree with M. André Maurois's comment, that Hugo had by nature the gift of portraying the gigantic, the excessive, the theatrical and the panoramic, and is justified by the truth and nobility of his feelings. Our difficulty is that we can nowadays recognise, by general psychological aid and the torture chambers of contemporary history, the monstrous side of a book like *Notre-Dame de Paris*, but have disconnected it from the ideal. We can recognise horror and grotesque, and even respond to the rhetoric of darkness; we are unable to credit the rhetoric of light. We are too absorbed in the rediscovery of evil. For Hugo, the black and white artist, one could not exist without the other. He was a primitive in that respect—or a commercial.

In *Notre-Dame de Paris* Hugo's dreams are magnified in outline, microscopic in detail. They are true but are made magical by the enlargement of pictorial close-up, not by grandiloquent fading. Compare the treatment of the theme of the love that survives death in this book with the not dissimilar theme in *Wuthering Heights*. Catherine and Heathcliffe are eternal as the wretched wind that whines at the northern casement. They are impalpable and bound in their eternal pursuit. A more terrible and more precise fate is given by Hugo to Quasimodo after death. The hunchback's skeleton is found clasping the skeleton of the gypsy girl in the charnel house. We see it with our eyes. And his skeleton falls into dust when it is touched, in that marvellous last line of the novel. Where love is lost, it is lost even beyond the grave. The reader is made to see this finality with his own eyes. If we object that Hugo's world is rhetorical, his scepticism, irony and wit give the rhetoric earth to stand on. Quasimodo is put to the torture in a ferocious scene, but it follows a trial which is based on the stock sardonic comedy of deaf prisoner at odds with deaf judge. The novel is a romance, but its parts exist in equilibrium. Interwoven with the tragedians—Quasimodo, the girl, the lusting priest—is the pedestrian Gringoire who has been quick to make his peace with the world, like some Shakespearean clown. He grows before our eyes, as all the characters grow. Beginning as a bore, he becomes the nervous smile on the face of that practical pusillanimity which we call the common experience and the instinct to survive. (We live by our genius for hope; we survive by our talent for dispensing with it. Turning to M. Maurois's *Life* and recognising that part of Hugo's greatness lay in his efficiency in using every item of his life, we wonder if Gringoire was some malicious version of a Sainte-Beuve, for he has married the Muse platonically. He will be a critic.) "What makes you so attached to your life?" the haunted archdeacon asks him. Gringoire makes the gracious Pyrrhonian reply about the sun, flowers, birds and books and adds the sublime sentence: "And then I have the happiness of spending every day, from morning to night, in the company of a man of genius, myself. It is very pleasant."

Hugo was the impresario of a split personality. Out of the depths came the monsters created by chastity: lust, cruelty, jealousy, violence, maiming, murder, in pursuit of the innocent, the loving and the merciful. The black and white view is relieved by the courage of the priest's feckless brother and the scepticism of Gringoire, the whole is made workable by poetic and pictorial instinct. It has often been pointed out that Hugo had the eye that sees for itself. Where Balzac described things out of descriptive gluttony, so that parts of his novels are an undiscriminating buyer's catalogue; where Scott describes out of antiquarian zeal, Hugo brings things to life by implicating them with persons in the action in rapid "takes". In this sense, *Notre-Dame de Paris* was the perfect film script. Every stone plays its part. We can be sure the bells of Notre-Dame are not there merely to ring; they will act upon a life; and, in fact, they deafen Quasimodo and that deafness ruins him in the courts, saves him and ruins him in love. In *Les Misérables* we can be sure Hugo does not describe, say, the inn sign at the Thénaudiers' out of sheer love of describing inn signs; a volume later Thénaudier turns up with it, in another setting, trying to palm it off as a picture by David. Once we have caught on to this clinching habit of Hugo's, every scene springs to action. We are waiting for the magic to work. Sometimes the trick is too obvious: we know the dancing girl will find her mother by matching her shoe. "The reader will have guessed"—a ham phrase often repeated, but therein lies half the pleasure. We *have* guessed, as we guess in magic.

More important than this, for the critic, is the fact that Hugo's simplifications of the inner life are required by a superb sense of the theatre. He works entirely within its terms. One can see where he was trained. He works by stage scenes. The scene before Notre-Dame is a stage set. He has the art of placing a situation, opposing an obstacle, creating a new situation, reversing it, doubling and redoubling. Rushing in the dark to save the gypsy in the tower of the cathedral from her attacker, Quasimodo triumphs in his strength, but when he discovers the attacker is his master, the priest, all his will and strength collapse. Yet if the priest wins that round he loses it because of the new situation; it is he, the master, who has the bitterness of being enslaved. Not merely by lust for the girl, but by the new thing—jealousy of his hunchback servant. Hugo was popular but not necessarily false because he put the obsessive and strong situations in simple theatrical terms. He is rich in dramatic irony. There is a purely stage scene where Louis IX inspects at length the construction of a wooden cage in which a prisoner is wailing for mercy. The king does not notice the prisoner because, in his avarice, he is too interested in the cost of the wood. Yet when another prisoner appeals for mercy the king lets him off out of whim. Fate rules us all, the Wheel of Fortune is a trickster. Hugo's whole method as a novelist is contained in these dramatic ironies and reversals, but he applies it in such a variety of ways and at so many levels that we do not notice the mechanics of it. In story-telling the method has the immense advantage of a delaying tactic: see the manner in which the dreadful Thénaudier in *Les Misérables* is made to reveal his adroitness, chance by chance. And if we ask ourselves whether Hugo's characters live outside the theatre, Thénaudier provides one answer. Hugo has to see them in that spotlight in order to see them truthfully at all.

A typical passage of Ciceronian oratory on Thénaudier's wickedness ends with the typical epigram which contains a truth: in this wicked man there was "*quelque chose qui était hidieux comme le mal et poignant comme le vrai*". The ideal world is a world of opposites; in the rhetorical evocation of it, it is the last short sentence of the harangue that makes the dramatic point and clinches the scene. Hugo never fails with that sentence. The old dying Jacobin denounces the church like an orator for pages on end and, for reply, the saintly Abbé simply kneels and says: "Give me your blessing." That is good theatre, for it does not make the priest theatrical; it convinces us that he is alive. One has to admit that Hugo can overdo it. In the very next line, the old Jacobin falls back dead. That is too much. The critics who warned Hugo of his excess of originality and of his weakness for doubling his metaphors and his points, were right; at a deeper level there is the objection that a love of paradox is likely to turn into the high-flown belief that everything equals everything in the end. (Which one is pursuer, which pursued: Javert or Valjean?) But the highest moment of an art so ingeniously staged in its particulars is not metaphysics but spectacle. The attack on Notre-Dame by the army of beggars; the preparations for the execution of the gypsy girl and her escape; the scenario of Waterloo—these are all crises on the grand scale and classical operatic instances of the mass scene.

The fact that Hugo's characters are larger than life as individuals and are only life-size when they are part of a crowd—judges, soldiers, beggars, populace—does not mean, of course, that they are not individual and recognisable, or even that they are either allegorical or caricature. There are no unconvincing or sentimentalised characters in *Notre-Dame* or *Les Misérables*, as there are in Scott. (The two novelists are not really comparable; it would be more sensible to call Hugo "incurious Dostoevsky" rather than "inferior Scott".

Hugo was simply too extroverted to know how morbid the sources of some of his ideas were; he merely knew that they drove his brother mad, not himself.) If *Les Misérables* is a lesser and more ambitious work than *Notre-Dame*, this is partly because it is humourless and has little comedy. But Hugo's genius was for the creation of simple and recognisable myth. The huge success of *Les Misérables* as a didactic work on behalf of the poor and oppressed is due to its poetic and myth-enlarged view of human nature—intermingled with that fundamental regard for human cunning which a popular culture seems to call for. Hugo himself called this novel "a religious work"; and it has indeed the necessary air of having been written by God in one of his more accessible and saleable moods. Myth and theatre, rather than fact and dogma, are what have made Quasimodo, Valjean, Javert universal in popular esteem. It is remarkable that the eight hundred superfluous pages of digression did not wreck the book.

TROLLOPE WAS RIGHT

THE comfort we get from Trollope's novels is the sedative of gossip. It is not cynical gossip, for Trollope himself is the honest check on the self-deceptions of his characters, on their malicious lies or interested half-truths about each other. It is he, a workaday surrogate of God, sincere, sturdy, shrewd and unhopeful, who has the key. Trollope does not go with us into the dangerous region that lies just outside our affairs and from which we draw our will to live; rather, he settles lazily into that part of our lives which is a substitute, the part which avoids loneliness by living vicariously in other people. If it is a true generalisation—as some say—that the English, being unimaginative, are able to live without hope but not without the pleasure of thinking they are better than their neighbours, Trollope's are the most English of our novels. But the generalisation is not true. Trollope himself—as Mr Cockshut says in a very intelligent study—is saved by eccentricity. There is something fervent, even extreme, in his admiration of endurance. He was a man whose temper could flare up. His preoccupation with what is normal is the intense one of a man who has had to gain acquaintance with normality from an abnormal situation outside it. His special eccentricities are his mania for work and his passion for spending energy. From his point of view, novel-writing was obsessional. It convinced him that he, the outsider in a society of powerful groups of people, was justified in being alive. Even his most contented novels leave an aftertaste of flatness and sadness. He has succeeded in his assertions, to the point of conveying a personal satiety.

The plots of Trollope and Henry James have much in common. But if we compare a novel like *The Eustace Diamonds*, one of the most ingenious of Trollope's conundrums, with, say, Henry James's *The Spoils of Poynton*, we see the difference between a pragmatic gossip and an artist of richer sensibility. Sense, not sensibility, governs Trollope; it is fine good sense and, though he lumbers along, most notable for the subtlety of its timing. He is an excellent administrator and politician of private life. But whereas James saw how the magnificent spoils of the Poynton family could corrupt by their very beauty, Trollope did not envisage anything morally ambiguous in the imbroglio of the Eustace diamonds. The *Spoils* were treasure; the *Diamonds* are property. The former are made for the moral law; the latter for the courts. It is true, as Mr Cockshut says, that the brilliantly delayed climax where Dove, the lawyer, points out the stones are worthless, has its overtones. But to Trollope's imagination the diamonds are ultimately meaningless; one might defend the wicked Lady Eustace and say that she alone gave them a symbolical meaning. They at least stand for her will. But Trollope in fact dislikes her childish will as much as her propensity for lying; her poetic side is shown to be false. One wonders if he could have portrayed it if it had been genuine. She is a perjurer, a bitch and a coquette and, quite rightly, ends up as a bore; but in a novel filled with irritable and spiritless people, she is the one figure of spirit. Trollope merely knows that she is wrong.

With all his mastery, Trollope is interested only in what people are like, not in what they are for. The limitation comes out most clearly in his political novels when we see how politics work and never for what purpose, beyond those of personal career. Some critics have put down this fundamental concern of Trollope to his good-natured and sensible acceptance of mid-Victorian society, and would say that he accepted his world just as Jane Austen accepted hers. Others—and I think Mr Cockshut would be among them—point to his constitutional melancholy. It has the effect of devitalising his characters. I do not mean that old harridans like Lady Linlithgow, the delightful self-willed Lady Glencora, or Lord George in *The Eustace Diamonds* lack personal vitality; the deficiency is in artistic vitality. If we compare the portrait of Lady Eustace with Thackeray's Becky Sharp it is interesting to see how much passivity there is in Lady Eustace and how much greater is the adventuress than the stubborn fool. Lady Eustace drifts. Her wickednesses are many, but they are small. She is little more than a tedious *intrigante* who relies on chance. She, of course, succeeds with us because of her obstinacy, her wit, her courage, her seductiveness and her beauty and because her wickedness is that of a child. Indeed Lord George, the "corsair", pats her on the head and treats her as such. Becky is a more positive and interesting figure of evil because she is grown up.

In *The Eustace Diamonds*, there are only two moments when Trollope breaks through his melancholy to write out of strong feeling. The first is an unpleasant outbreak: the anti-semitism of his portrait of Mr Emilius, "the greasy Jew". Trollope, honest observer that he is, notes that Lady Eustace is far from being physically repelled by the preacher who is said to be repulsive. The female masochist—as Mr Cockshut says—has recognised a master, the coquette her master-hypocrite. The second outbreak occurs in describing the brutal, forced engagement of Lucinda Roanoke to Sir Griffin, and the violence with which the Amazon repels him when he tries to take her on his knee. Here the revulsion is physical. These are two disconcerting glimpses into the Trollopian alcove and both are blatant. Trollope with his blood up is better seen on the hunting field; he will be kinder there to the women who are to be humiliated.

Mr Cockshut has read the whole of Trollope and I have

not. His book provides an able analysis of the novels and a fresh approach to Trollope himself. The critic might have said, with advantage, more about Trollope's curious life; Mr Cockshut is more detailed than other critics have been about Trollope's response to mid-Victorianism; he is fascinated by the moral issues which Trollope propounded, but he is apt to digress. As a critic he depends on paraphrase which is always suggestive and enjoyable though it also runs into the danger of crediting a novelist with ideas he may only dimly have discerned. Is it true, for example, that masochism is Lady Eustace's central characteristic? Surely it is a lack of interest in truth. Mr Cockshut's main point is that there are three phases in Trollope's prodigious output; the day-dream stage; the genial middle period when he accepts the world; and the final one, beginning with *He Knew He Was Right*, when he is bitterly disillusioned about the society which he has affirmed his right to. Mr Cockshut cannot think of any special reason for the change. Perhaps Trollope's leaving the Post Office and failing to get into Parliament had something to do with it. Leisure depressed, indeed terrified him and, perhaps, what Mr Cockshut calls his "belated understanding of the changes that were coming over Victorian England" became unpleasantly observable with leisure. We need not think that hard work exhausted him, but men who are hard on themselves become harder on other people as time goes by. "He knew he was right" could have been his device, the rightness not lying especially in his opinion, but in his choice of what might be called "practical hallucination" as a way of living. He was perhaps reverting in late middle age to the misanthropy of his early, unhappy youth. The cycle is common enough. Dickens, too, became harsh and, to present-day taste, the harsh or obsessional phase of novelists happens to have become attractive.

He Knew He Was Right and *The Eustace Diamonds* are not

genial books. There is something savage in them. The values of society are rotten, the people are fools, brutes or lunatics. Lady Eustace may be bad; but what are we to say of the virtuous Mrs Hittaway, the social climber, who does not scruple in the name of virtue to employ Lady Eustace's servants to spy upon her and who is so morally exalted by her own slanders that she does not even want to consider the evidence for them? These people are a nasty, grubbing lot, no better than they should be. Their story is redeemed and 'placed' by Trollope's smiling remark that the scandal managed to keep the old Duke of Omnium alive for three months and gave everybody in London something to talk about at dinner. Trollope may be pessimistic, but he was too alert a comedian to be misled into rancour. His good nature was truthful if it grew less and less hopeful. Himself morbidly subject to loneliness and boredom and capable of portraying characters who were destroyed by these evils, he never fell into exaggeration —nor indeed rose to it.

The Eustace Diamonds is a triumph of ingenious construction and of story-telling. Trollope is a master of that dramatic art which the English novel seems to have inherited from its early roots in the theatre; the art of putting the right in the wrong and the wrong in the right. He also understands Society and the difference between the weary meaninglessness of the conventional and the vicious aimlessness of the unconventional. The fast set and Grundys such as Mrs Hittaway, are opposite sides of the same coin. Yet if, as Mr Cockshut's analysis patiently shows, the gossip is morally organised, it is not schematic. The characters are various in themselves. A dull man like Lord Fawn becomes fascinating. We see the figure of Frank Greystock in all the colours of a merely moderate honesty. Each character is brought to its own dramatic head. Will Greystock jilt the governess and marry Lady Eustace? Trollope is not content to stop at answering that question, but goes one better and shows Greystock falling asleep in the train, bored stiff by a flirt who had captivated him. Trollope's observation can make even a Commissioner of Police interesting. Nor does the comedy remain on one level. The love affair of Lucinda and Sir Griffin approaches the grotesque and the horrible and the sharp financial deals and recriminations of Lady Eustace and Mrs Carbuncle are as savage as anything in *Jonathan Wild*. Trollope is a remorseless exploiter of fine points. If he had been a mere plot-maker he would have been satisfied to expose the perjuries of Lady Eustace in the court scene, but he squeezes more than that out of it. He sees to it that a sadistic counsel, powerless to be other than cruel, makes the liar tell the truth a dozen times over, unnecessarily. And when the bogus preacher proposes, Lady Eustace doubts if he is bogus enough.

The critic must admire these skills. He must admire Trollope's knowledge of the groups in the social hierarchy. He must notice how fertilising was Trollope's own dilemma: that he was a man of liberal mind crossed by strong conservative feeling. There remain the serious limitations that his manner is slovenly, repetitive and pedestrian, that his scene has no vividness, that—as Mr Cockshut says—the upper steps of his moral stairway are missing, that he lacks fantasy. There will be sin but no sanctity. It is, after all, Lady Eustace's crime that she was not the average woman and it is supposed to be Mrs Hittaway's justification that she is. And so, when we emerge from Trollope's world, we, at first, define him as one of the masters who enables us to recognise average life for what it is. On second thoughts, we change the phrase: we recognise that he has drawn life as people say it is when they are not speaking about themselves.

One of the chronicler's "failures"—*The Prime Minister*—was the penultimate volume of what Trollope considered his best work: the series which begins with *Can You Forgive Her?*

and runs on to the Phineas novels. As Mr Amery says in his introduction to the attractive Oxford Crown edition, it raises the question of politics in the novel. The failure of *The Prime Minister* is, of course, relative; no novel containing Lady Glencora could be called dull. But this one has no personable young hero like the frank and susceptible Phineas Finn and Emily Wharton is a bit of a stick as the meek but obstinate young bride in love. On the other hand, Lopez, the speculator and fortune-hunter, is a genuine figure of the age; drama is created by his shifty fingers, he is bold and credible. The only bother with Lopez is that he is made the vehicle of Trollope's peculiar dislike of "outsiders" and foreigners—he loathed Disraeli really because he was a Jew—and a hostile lecturing tone comes into Trollope's voice when he writes of him, which is absent from the portrait of that other rapscallion, Burgo Fitzgerald. Yet Trollope tries very hard to be fair to Lopez, who is presented with objective care and is never all of a piece. He has courage, for example, and one notices that he does not lie until he is kicked when he is down. Only his suicide, at the end, is out of character, for obviously a man like Lopez will always start again from the bottom. He perfectly illustrates what a novelist like Galsworthy would have made a lot of moral fuss about: that in a rich oligarchic society, the Lopezes will always be sacrificed when their heads are turned or when it is a question of class-solidarity and self-defence. Trollope is very accurate as a psychologist of the uncomprehending rogue; a little cynical as he shows how mad it is to think of succeeding in England if you use your imagination and disobey the rules. It is a tremendous moment when Lopez attempts to blackmail the Duke of Omnium and the best kind of surprise: the brilliant Lopez has lost his head. We had forgotten how stupid cleverness can be. Finally, in the major conflict between the lofty-minded Prime Minister and his wife, Lady Glencora, whose whole idea is to exploit her husband's political eminence socially, there is wit, and drama too.

Where is the specific failure, then? I do not mean the general criticism of Trollope that he is commonplace, that reading him is like walking down endless corridors of carpet, restful to walk on, but in the end enervating. What is the failure within Trollope's own honest terms? The reader is bound to agree with the experienced opinion of the politician who introduces the book: as Mr Amery says, it was possible for Trollope to write about the Church without engaging in religious controversy, because this is only fitful in religion and, anyway, is only one aspect of it. But controversy is the living breath of politics, and Trollope leaves it out altogether. He purposely makes the Duke of Omnium Prime Minister of a Coalition, in which controversy is momentarily quiet. The fact is that Trollope the civil servant despised politicians and the Duke of Omnium is really a Treasury official, plus an immense sense of rank and a vast income. And so, though we hear in detail of the machinery of Parliament, the intrigues for safe seats, the machinations of the drawing-rooms and have an excellent picture of political comedy and humbug, we have no notion of politics as anything more than a career disputed between the "ins" and the "outs".

It infuriated Trollope to see that Disraeli's political novels were more highly thought of than his own. He wrote of them:

> Through it all there is a feeling of stage properties, a smell of hair-oil, an aspect of buhl, a remembrance of tailors, and that pricking of the conscience which must be the general accompaniment of paste diamonds.

Even so, Disraeli's *Sybil* and *Coningsby* are far more convincing as political novels. They burn with the passions of the day and if there is falsity in the lighting, that is an essential political quality. Disraeli presents politics as prophetic dogma; he understands that politics grow out of beliefs, interests and conditions, though they degenerate into expedients. The working class are not excluded as Trollope excludes them; and though Trollope lived in a quieter political period, it can hardly be said that the workers were without voice. Disraeli's vision of politics in his novels was exotic and perhaps no purely English novelist is capable of this, any more than he has been capable of the dialectical fantasies of Shaw; to write well about politics one has got to believe in them in the abstract and to regard them as a possible imaginative world. Trollope hated the idea of such a thing, and in consequence, though he gets the surface brilliantly, he misses the reason for its existence.

Character is the whole interest of Trollope and if his portrait of the Prime Minister, the Duke of Omnium, is meant to be a picture of the perfect gentleman and statesman, it is neither idealised nor forced. The Duke's skin is too thin, he has scruples, he is moody, morose and capable of ducal temper. Though he is in conflict with his wife, who gives a fantastic house party—40 guests a night for six weeks, and none to stay more than 48 hours; think, says the housekeeper at Gatherum Castle, as if she had Arnold Bennett at her elbow, of the towels and the sheets!—the Duke clearly understands that if she is a woman with no scruples, she is kept straight by her feelings and convictions. And Trollope is expert in crossing the intentions of his people with the accidents of life. The climber Lopez might have got his safe seat, if only the bumptious Major Pountney—"a middle-aged young man"—had not annoyed the Duke on another matter. But we get, I think, a better idea of the political entanglement in the earlier book, *Phineas Finn*. Phineas is not an outsider, and therefore Trollope is in a better temper. He is the ingenious, penniless, handsome young fellow, going into politics against the author's affectionate advice and we are led with him step by step into his career. There are even glances at the

Irish Question. We see Phineas funking his first opportunity to speak and making a mess of it when he does get up, full of indignation, on another occasion.

There are shrewd portraits of the Whips—but there is nothing to equal Disraeli's wonderful libellous sketch of Croker—and Trollope knows how to grade his politicians according to the condition of their careers. There is a hostile portrait of John Bright. He is Turnbull, who is contrasted with Monk, an imaginary Radical "ever doubting of himself, and never doubting himself so much as when he had been most violent and also most effective, in debate". But Turnbull-Bright has no doubts:

> I think that when once he had learned the art of arranging his words as he stood on his legs, and had so mastered his voice as to have obtained the ear of the House, the work of his life was not difficult. Having nothing to construct he could always deal with generalities. Being free from responsibility, he was not called upon either to study details or to master even great facts. It was his business to inveigh against existing evils, and perhaps there is no easier business. . . . It was his work to cut down forest trees, and he had nothing to do with the subsequent cultivation of the land. Mr Monk had once told Phineas Finn how great were the charms of that inaccuracy which was permitted to the opposition.

That is all very well, but the very irony at the expense of politicians shows the failure to rise to the imaginative opportunity. As Mr Amery says, Disraeli would have plunged for the excitements of foreign policy. He would have risked.

Indeed, although *Phineas Finn* is an amusing guide to Parliamentary life as it then was, it interests us really for things like the famous portraits of the violent red-eyed Lord Chiltern—this plunging, dangerous man would be the hero of a contemporary novel, not a minor character—the superb

Mr Kennedy, so gloomy, so evangelical, who adroitly lengthens family prayers when he is jealous of his wife's lover:

> [He] was a man who had very little temptation to do anything wrong. He was possessed of over a million and a half of money, which he was mistaken enough to suppose he had made himself. . . . He never spoke much to anyone, although he was constantly in society. He rarely did anything, though he had the means of doing everything. He had seldom been on his legs in the House of Commons, though he had been there ten years. He was seen about everywhere, sometimes with one acquaintance, sometimes with another—but it may be doubted whether he had any friend . . . though he would not lend money, he gave a great deal—and he would give it for almost every object. "Mr Rbt. Kennedy, M.P., £105" appeared on almost every charitable list that was advertised. No one ever spoke to him as to this expenditure, nor did he ever speak to anyone. Circulars came to him and the cheques were returned. The duty was an easy one to him and he performed it willingly. Had any moment of inquiry been necessary it is possible the labour would have been too much for him.

That is a close study of something not often observed: the neutrality, the nonentity of rich men. And then there are the women of the book who all talk so well and who are very well distinguished from each other. The stress on sex in the modern novel has meant that women have lost their distinctiveness as persons. Trollope excels in making the distinctions clear.

Trollope is a detailed, rather cynical observer of a satisfied world. Honest, assertive, sensible, shrewd, good-humoured, he is content. As Henry James said, he gives us the pleasure of recognition. But content is, so to speak, a summit that he has attained, not a torpor into which he has fallen. He grew worldliness like a second skin over the raw wounds of his youth, and the reason why he describes what is normally observable about people so well, is that he longed merely for the normal. He had been too insecure to want anything more than that security, and it was by a triumph of personal character that he attained it. Trollope might excusably have become a neurotic—and without talent. It is maddening to see the themes of Henry James taken back to the platitude of their starting point and left there; strange to have to recognise that what are called "things as they are" can be soothing. It is dangerous to marry for money, but it is also dangerous to marry for love; it is dangerous to commit adultery for society will drop you, yet society is greedy and hypocritical. It is bad to borrow; it is mean not to lend. One is listening to human nature muddling along on its old rules of thumb. The only pattern we can discern is that made by the struggle of the individual within his group: politics, the law, the Church. It is not a passionate struggle. It is mainly a question of faintly enlightened self-interest. We feel about his people what we feel about our relatives: the curiosity that distracts us from a fundamental apathy. The sense of danger and extremity which alerts us in the war-like compositions of Jane Austen, is dulled. His novels are social history, without the movements of history; life as we see it without having to think about it. It has no significance beyond itself; it is as pleasant, dull and restful as an afternoon in an armchair. The footpads in the London parks, the frightened family of the crooked bankrupt, the suicide on the suburban line, are there, not to frighten us unduly, but to give further assurance to normal people that normality is stronger than ever. Can we wonder, in these times, at the Trollope revival?

ROSS AT THE DEPOT

WITHHELD from the public in the 'twenties when it was written, T. E. Lawrence's *The Mint* is one of those time-bombs of literature which fail to go off when the hour comes. Its mystery, kept alive by a leak here and there, a single copy circulating somewhere or other, and by people "privileged to see", had been artificial; and the habit of building up expectation of "revelations" in his work was maintained even on publication, in 1955, by issuing an unexpurgated edition in leather at extra cost. It is an odd comment on our manners that we have contrived to make the short list of four-letter words, on which an army moves, into the nuggets of a publisher's gold-mine. Lawrence was, of course, writing when the revival of the rights of blasphemy and bad language was regarded as an ethical duty; but, for a later generation, military service and war have not been a novelty, linguistically or otherwise, and I doubt whether anyone under forty will want to pay to read exactly what the soldier said so often. No scandal, no sex, no sodomy. *The Mint* is simply an earnest documentary work. It was noted down night after night in the Nissen huts of the R.A.F. Depot, records what went on in the huts and on the square and what it felt like to have one's spirit broken and to be turned into 352087 A/c Ross. This experience has become a commonplace to the majority of living males and dozens of documentaries have described the process. In waiting till 1955 the book has waited too long and discloses nothing much about Lawrence himself.

All the same, there is a curious period interest in *The Mint*.

It is an arty book: Lawrence's own injured romanticism and his self-pity see to that. One sees now a pathos in the stilted originality which was worked into so much of the more ardent prose of the time and which I take to be a hangover from Meredith.

> So the appellant moon easily conjures me outside. . . . On the western slope swelled the strident activity of red-and-chocolate footballers.

Lawrence's prose attempts to attract attention to its airs and merits; he is a word prig. Occasionally, in a portrait, an eventual touch of fantasy justifies him:

> China . . . is a stocky Camberwell costermonger, with the accent of a stage Cockney. Since childhood he has fought for himself and taken many knocks, but no care about them. He is sure that safety means to be rough among the town's roughs. His deathly white face is smooth as if waxed, the bulging pale eyes seem lidless like a snake's, and out of their fixedness he stares balefully. . . . China has said, "F——" so often, inlaying it monotonously after every second word of his speech with so immense an aspirated "f", that his lips have pouted to it in a curve which sneers across his face like the sound-hole of a fiddle's belly.

It must be said that *The Mint* is more laboured in its first painful 165 pages, which are based on notes taken certainly too close to the object; the remaining forty pages, based on letters, are both happier in themselves and are more freely written. (This part of the book contains an excellent description of speeding on a motor bike.) Lawrence wrote spiritedly about action. Another virtue of *The Mint* lies in its honest effort to get to the bottom of his subject. At first the impression is that what is unique experience for him in his egocentric way is commonplace for his fellows, but presently he notices that it will not be commonplace for them either. In 1923, with a million and a half unemployed in England, enlistment meant the open acknowledgment of defeat by life. Having lost their souls, men glumly hesitated as they handed over their last possession: their bodies.

> We include "lads" and their shady equivalent, the hard case. Also the soft and the silly: the vain: the old soldier who is lost without the nails of service: the fallen officer sharply contemptuous of our new company, yet trying to be well-fellow and not proud. Such a novice dips too willingly at the dirty jobs, while the experienced wage-slave stands by, grumbling.
>
> The dressy artisans, alternately allured and repelled by our unlimited profession, dawdle for days over their trade-tests, hoping some accident will make up their minds. Our Glasgow blacksmith given only bread and tea one day in dining hall, cried, "Aam gaen whame," muddled his trial job and was instantly turned down. That last afternoon he spent spluttering crazy, non-intelligible confidences at every one of us. A dumpy lad he was, with tear-stained fat cheeks, and so glad to have failed. "Dry bread," he would quiver half-hourly with a sob in his throat. Simple-minded, like a child, but stiff-minded, too, and dirty; very Scotch.

Lawrence himself joined the R.A.F. under the name of Ross at a time of physical and spiritual exhaustion in his life when (he said) he was capable of only negative decisions. He wanted, he says, to get back to human kind and, half-way through the book, he thinks the plan has failed. It probably did fail: it was loveless and despairing. The malicious and the knowing have described Lawrence's enlistment as an example of his chronic play-acting, but human motives are rarely simple; even if he were play-acting, this is as serious and complex a compulsion as its opposite, and not less "real" or "sincere". Self-dramatisation is common among gifted men and provides its own experience. At the Air Force medical, the doctor noted, Lawrence says (no doubt with some self-infatuation) that he looked as though he had been going short of food for months. If he had, there was no need for him to have done, and he may have half-starved in a sulking desire to show he had not received sufficient attention. That does not alter the fact that a hungry man was abasing himself before the doctor. The theme of abasement already occurs in *The Seven Pillars of Wisdom*; in *The Mint* one is struck by the analogy with religious conversion. The book might indeed be a histrionic footnote to Alfred de Vigny's elaborate comparison of the religious and military vocations. The world is abandoned, and the gates close on the recruit. As private possessions, the body and the mind are systematically destroyed, the will is thrown away, the subject is in a condition as abject as that of Saint Ignatius when he stood in rags at Montserrat; only after abasement can obedience become an instinct and the old man give place to the new man, the required automaton, fulfilled in corporate pride and corporate wholeness. That is the ultimate reward; in the interim, he sinks restfully and unresponsibly into the dull, kind, corrupt world of the closed community, where promiscuousness kills the desire for intimacy, where sex is a dirty word, and the last feeble ghosts of private life escape in groans and babblings from the lips in sleep at night. That is purgatory. It is a loss that Lawrence had to leave the R.A.F.: the will to describe the experiences of the technician's heaven vanished.

To his companions, as far as so impersonal a writer can disclose it, Lawrence was an oddity. He could not swear. They were considerate about his age—he was eight years older than most and was physically exhausted more quickly than they. They admired his use of long words, they borrowed a little money. They must have seen him wince at the sight of their bullocky animality. He let them down in one respect: every man has some small advantage he can exploit; why, as a "toff", did he not exploit the fact? There was no masochism in the men, there was no point in being a "mug". This complaint came to a head in the conflict with a sergeant who was one of two or three sadists who made his life hell at the Depot in those days. This sergeant was a killer. One day, when he had reduced his squad to a helpless, gasping collection of sweating and frightened animals, he made a short inspection to finish them off, stopped in front of Lawrence and said: " 'When did you have a bath? Open your collar,' thrust his hand roughly inside against my wet breast. 'Christ, the bloody man's lousy. . . . March the filthy —— out to the wash-house and scrub the —— out of him properly.' " Lawrence was marched off by Sailor, who had a great command of picturesque obscenity. The blanks lengthen in Sailor's dialogue: "God if that long —— streak of —— pokes his head in here after us, I'll knock seven different sorts of —— out of him. But, mate, you let the flight down, when he takes the mike out of you every time. Give the ignorant —— -bag a —— great gob of your toffology."

Pain is the subject of *The Mint* and it is not pain quietly borne. It is relieved by rough kindness. When Lawrence, who slept badly, went for a walk at night he was treated with sympathy, wonder and pity by the sentries. He observed their new character growing up in the men. Once the hell of drill was over and they got to the machines, they found the unconscious solace of mass men: the machines belonged to them, not to the silly fools who flew them and messed them up. Lawrence was moved by this, and the puritan in him responded to the dull-self-righteousness of unexceptional people. Since he was exceptional himself he must have been divided in mind. It is pretty evident that he knew he had no place there and that the cure—that old, mystical, muddled notion of "going back to the people"—was, stunt or no stunt, a failure. The affair of the motor bicycle suggests the trouble was one that could not be solved by immolation in the corporate life. And there *The Mint* leaves us. It is, in point of writing, one of the first documentaries, tortuous and self-conscious, vivid and affected, powerful and yet weakened by shrillness and mannered introspection. Writing was not his medium. Or, rather, to be his medium it had to have the great, cruel, false, personal, romantic subject, with Carlyle's "dark curtains" coming down on it in the end. The Royal Air Force was precisely not that in 1923 and, in seeing the commonest men only in relation to their failure in civilian life and their military training, he showed his distance from them. Those writers who have succeeded in portraying common men have not made them the acolytes of the writer's own personal rituals. One is left, at the end of *The Mint*, moved by the writer's pain and nagged by the peculiarity of his case. One is not left with very much more.

THE MILITARY NECESSITY

IT has taken nearly one hundred and twenty years for Alfred de Vigny's apologia for the military life to come once more into its own. It has had to wait for the tide of peace to turn and for the birth of two war generations. Like some writers of our own 'twenties, Vigny had imagined that negotiation was bound to succeed war in the diplomacy of nations and that science would eventually bring in the world state and make war impossible. He did not see that it would make war more alluring and interesting. Yet his accent is persuasive when he expresses this feeling, for he had the art of keeping rational hope faint but alive and of surrounding it with compassion for its insignificance. A lesson to propagandists: the pessimism which addresses itself to the last feeble spark of reason in our minds has a longer life than the bullying good will which slaps and pushes us along. From our point of view Vigny's personal aloofness and melancholy hit the mark. Mr Humphrey Hare, who has made an excellent translation, says that Vigny was never temperamentally at home in the circumstances of his life which were, indeed, generally dejecting, and that the crisis of the Revolution seemed to be "perpetually alive in him". He was not born until 1797 but his mind was formed by the eighteenth century, his parents were aristocrats whose property was sequestered, and although he was brought up to the idea of military glory, he was also taught that Bonaparte was an impostor. His coldness and remoteness were the formal mask of the man who finds himself between two worlds, but they were not the Byronic mask of a "doomed" or "lost" generation, for Vigny was a natural stoic who understood abnegation and pity. He had little egoism. He astonished and amused people like Dumas and Hugo by his fastidiousness—his mistress said she had only once seen him eat, and then only a carrot; as a soldier, he treated the army stiffly, as a "nomad monastery", a place for order, solitude, contemplation and self-effacement. Sainte-Beuve mocked him for being a Trappist and Vigny himself put down his failure in the army to having brought a passive and reflective mind to an active avocation. Vocation it certainly was not.

Vigny had an aristocratic dignity, the sense that Duty is Fate. This gave him a backbone which is lacking in the other disillusioned Romantics. When he occasionally falls into their inflated manner he writes poorly. "In the universal foundering of creeds", which was felt in his time, as it has been in ours, he believed in the aristocratic and "earthly religion" of honour: "the virtue of the life of this world." The argument and the stories that make up *The Military Necessity* are based on this sense, and it enabled him to define the moral essence of a soldier's life and the tragic mutilation of the individual, humane soul by the corporate spirit. The key to his thought lies in his account of the explosion at Vincennes when the kindly over-zealous quartermaster is blown to pieces.

> Like a stone from a sling his head and torso had been hurled sixty feet up against the chapel wall, and the powder, impregnating this appalling bust, had cut its outline deeply on the wall at whose foot he had fallen back. Although we gazed at it for a long time, no one uttered a word of pity. Possibly because to have pitied him would have been to have pitied ourselves for having run the self-same danger.

Any society requires the inhibition of feeling in its members and Vigny's point is that this is inevitable, and perhaps desirable. But he also indicates the price that has to be paid: a loss of heart and above all a loss of compassion. We should feel most compassionate of all to the soldier who sacrifices himself to society's requirement that he shall have no compassion:

> The army is blind and dumb, strikes down unquestioningly those to whom it is opposed, desires nothing for itself and acts under compulsion. It is a great machine wound up to kill; but it is, too, a machine capable of suffering.

For Vigny the modern army is a "body divorced from the great body of the nation". It is the scapegoat. In his long time of service he was painfully sensitive to these definitions, because he himself saw no active service against a foreign enemy: the most he had to do was to help quell a riot of liberal citizens in the town of Pau. It was bad enough to be the licensed murderer abroad; but to have that role in one's own country was pathetic and false. (This is the situation Stendhal angrily described in *Lucien Leuwen*.) What Vigny is commemorating is the frustration of the old Napoleonic sense of glory—Napoleon appears unsympathetically in one of the stories in this book—the loss of romance.

Does the modern soldier still feel himself to be in a false position, in Vigny's sense? By 1914–18 he certainly did, but has the feeling continued in the conscripted, peace-time armies? Some have felt military service to be a happy return to their schooldays; but for most men the experience is that of the guinea-pig who is made to suffer the effects of a major psychological operation. Like the novice, he submits to mutilation in order to obtain a special kind of soul. Like the soldier of Vigny's time he is a man "thrown, changed, recast, shaped for ever to a common pattern. The man is lost in the soldier" —as he is lost in the monk. Routine, the check on the intelligence, reserve, obedience to artificial authority, bring out the melancholy and coarseness of boredom in military life; the gain, Vigny says, is abnegation and sacrifice:

> This utter abnegation of which I have been speaking, together with the constant and careless expectation of death, the complete renunciation of all liberty of thought and action, the delays, suffered by a limited ambition and the impossibility of acquiring riches, all produce virtues which are much rarer among those classes of men who remain free and independent.

A monastery, a prison, the chains gladly accepted—such are Vigny's metaphors. A stoical doctrine, yet if it is wisdom and even freedom to submit to Fate and to obey, this submission is as corrupting as the pride of the man who believes he is free. Vigny wrote as a soldier of the peace-time bodyguard and garrison; he did not know the passion of action except by hearsay and he was austerely, humourlessly unaware of the corruption of the bored camp. He himself wasted a large part of his life in a profession to which he was unsuited—except that it gave him this book.

As a personal document, in which the self is disciplined to the point of anonymity, *The Military Necessity* is a classically clear and direct piece of writing. It is originally conceived. Vigny is an artist-philosopher. He sets out his theme a little at a time and then breaks off to tell at leisure a story that illustrates it. The military argument is a frame, as Turgenev's after-dinner conversations were or Merimée's reflections on travel and custom, for three dramatic stories of character and action. This method of writing a short story will always attract the aspirant because it seems to be the easiest, for it gives the writer points of rest and provides him with the easy opportunity of stating an argument or a moral. The reader is deceived: for the requirement of this art is that one shall state a case without appearing to do so. Mr Humphrey Hare quotes Sainte-Beuve's praise of Vigny's poetry:

> He never . . . produces his tears as tears; he transforms them . . . If he wishes to give vent to the anguish of genius or to the loneliness of a poet's heart, he does not do so directly as would M. de Lamartine, with a lyrical effusion, instead he takes the indirect method.

Vigny is always concrete. He is various and resilient in feeling and in portraiture. The poor quartermaster is blown up at Vincennes but the tragic irony of this perfunctory death is effective because we had seen the old man in his youth, in his fairy-tale love affair, his love of homely music, in his fussing care and his fantastic life-long luck. Vigny has taken care to move us; his very arguments about the military life are feelings purged of personal rancour. His second virtue is that of surprise. When we meet the broken officer who is trailing through the mud of Flanders, with a mad girl in the cart behind him, we expect some tale of the misery of war, but it turns out to be far worse, an affair of political execution and the sea. The soldier has been ordered to shoot the girl's lover and he has saddled himself with his guilt. The officer with the malacca cane in the next story is similarly engaged in expiation. By doing their duty all his soldiers isolate themselves from humanity and accept a guilt which they cannot forget, and which is not "their fault". They are the martyrs of society. The event which causes this, in every case, is always astonishing, sudden and fearful.

Vigny has an exquisite sensibility to atmosphere and place. One will not easily forget the Flanders road, the attack on the Chateau at Reims, the simple barrack scenes at Vincennes or the long, dull, noiseless night in Paris deserted on the eve of the Revolution; such scenes have the supreme deceptive and allaying effect found only in the great story-tellers. What are those fires? The shopkeepers are merely burning down the trees that have darkened their shops; so does a revolution begin. It is on the day when nothing happens that everything happens. Then, at the critical moment of action, this quiet and reflective writer breaks into unforgettable physical detail. It is detail, uniquely of the occasion, which a writer of stories must always seek—the muddle of the execution at sea when the girl is put by mistake in full view of her lover's death; the terrible moment in *The Malacca Cane*, when Captain Renaud, afraid of being afraid, runs his sword into a body during the night-scrimmage at the Chateau:

> an elderly officer, a big strong man, though his hair was grey, rose like a ghost, uttered a fearful cry at the sight of what I had done, and thrusting violently at my face with a sword, fell instantly beneath the bayonets. I, too, fell to a sitting position beside him, stunned by a blow between the eyes, and I heard near me the dying voice of a child saying, "Papa."

Thus we know that Captain Renaud has killed a child, not a man, before its father's eyes. Or there is the dramatic eaves-dropping on the meeting of Napoleon and the Pope. These crises are burned in all their special detail upon the reader's mind, as the outline of the quartermaster's body was printed by blast on the wall. One never forgets the physical scene which has been exactly caught from the chaos of feeling by a cool artist.

The admirable thing in *The Military Necessity* is the novel and unobtrusive interweaving of story and argument. Again and again, when we think we are about to be fobbed off with an anecdote or a memory, we find Vigny going much further. Though the story of the malacca cane culminates in the episode at the Chateau, it has taken us through the life of Admiral Collingwood, through a consideration of the character of Bonaparte and the seductions and errors of the idea of glory. It has discussed whether we shall serve men or principles; it has discussed the dehumanisation of man; the acceptance of retribution; the fact that ultimately life will deny us justice.

We are always in deeper than we expect; we retrieve the idea of "the military necessity", just at the moment when it seemed forgotten and when false freedom seemed to be breaking in. The book does set up against the amorphous literature of our day the dramatic blessings of an original and ingenious sense of form, the value of a decisive sense not merely of material but of fundamental subject. The latter is what we lack today. Vigny's life suggests that subjects are best found by writers who submit themselves to an intolerable spiritual pressure.

THE MAJOR'S DAUGHTER

He was greatly mourned at the Curragh where his cattle were well-known; and all who had taken up his bets were particularly inconsolable for his loss to society.

THE quotation does not come from *The Irish R.M.*, but from the mother, or should one say the aunt, of the Anglo-Irish novel—Maria Edgeworth. The eighteenth-century note is unmistakable but so, even without the word Curragh, is the Irishness. One will never quite get to the bottom of that sentence out of *Castle Rackrent*. On the surface it is felt and good-natured. "Poor" Sir Kit, after hitting a toothpick out of his adversary's finger in a duel, received a ball in a vital part, and "was brought home in little better than an hour after the affair, speechless on a hand-barrow to my lady". A sad business; but landlords come and go; we know them by their debts; only cattle are eternal. Irish irony has been sharpened to a fine edge; it is more drastic than the corresponding irony of the English writers of the time. Sententious, secure in the collective, educated self-regard of their class, the English ironists regard folly from the strong point of cultivated applause and moral platitude, whereas an Irishwoman, like Maria Edgeworth, has uncertainty under foot. The folly of the death of Sir Kit is only equalled by the absurdity of the mourning; beyond both lies the hopeless disaster of the state of "the unfortunate country".

Behind an ironist like Fielding is assurance, courage and complacency; behind Maria Edgeworth, and Irish irony, lie indignation, despair, the political conscience. The rights and wrongs of Irish politics come into her works by implication.

We see the absentees, the rackrenters, the bought politicians, the English, Jewish, Scottish heiresses brought in to save colonial insolvency. We see the buffoon priests and the double-minded retainers. We do not see the rebellion, the boys hiding in the potato fields, but we do catch the tension. The clever, wise daughter of an enlightened father, a woman always ready to moralise about cause and effect in the neat eighteenth-century way, Maria Edgeworth was Irish enough to enjoy without shame the unreasonable climate of human temper and self-will, Irish enough to be generous about the genius for self-destruction. She was a good woman, ardent but —as Sir Walter Scott said—formidably observant, probably cool, perhaps not strong in sensibility; but she was not sentimental. Her irony—and surely this is Irish from Swift to Shaw—is the exploitation of folly by a reckless gaiety.

Castle Rackrent is the only novel of Maria Edgeworth's which can be read with sustained pleasure by the reader of today. Its verve and vivacity are as sharp as a fiddle's. It catches on like a jig; if it belongs to the artless time of the English novel, it is not clogged up by old-fashioned usage. I have never read *The Absentee*, which is often praised, but I have tried *Belinda*, a picture of the London smart set, and *Ormonde*. They, too, are vivacious, but there is not much point in finding time for them. They have a minor place in the history of the novel. One can only say that she has an original observation of men and women, an unspoiled eye for types; her moralisings are at any rate free from Victorian sentimentality, but are not in themselves interesting. Is it better for affection to follow esteem, or for esteem to follow affection? How are we to keep the peace between sensitiveness and sensibility, between the natural and the frivolous heart? How do we distinguish the line where generosity becomes self-indulgence? All this is good training, no doubt; but Maria Edgeworth was at her best when she was not being explicit about it. Character for its own sake, as the work of so many women novelists has shown, was the strong subject of this kind, clear-headed, irreverent woman, who never disturbs but also rarely comes to the foregone conclusion.

Belinda is a sharp-eyed tour of the London marriage market. No woman is less deceived by other women than this unsoured spinster who adored her father, wrote handbooks on education with him, managed his estate, "got on" with his four wives and looked after his twenty-one children. The Edgeworths were a nation in themselves. She could draw an old rip like Lady Delacour, a matchmaker like Mrs Stanhope pushing her débutantes, and a dangerous "metaphysical" woman like Lady Millicent in *Ormonde* with "the sweet persuasive voice and eloquent eyes—hers was a kind of exalted sentimental morality, referring everything to feeling, and to the notion of *sacrifice* . . . but to describe her notions she was very nearly unintelligible". Maria Edgeworth was the Major's daughter; the unintelligible was the unforgivable. It was very plain to her that the Lady Millicents of this world are so exalted that they do not know right from wrong. The men are as firmly drawn as the women. *Ormonde* contains a rich portrait of one of those hospitable, sociable, gallant, warm-hearted Irishmen, the souls of courtesy, whose imagination leads them into difficulties and ends by corrupting them, until the warm heart goes stone cold and they become the familiar Irish politician who will sell himself and anybody. Such a portrait might be done flat in bitterness and satire; Miss Edgeworth works in depth, engages our sympathy for the man, makes him captivate us—as he would in life—and gradually undeceives us without melodrama or ill-nature. None of these are great characters, but they are faithful observations of character. They are a truthful gallery, as capricious as life, of the figures of a class and an age. Such—we can be certain—was the life she knew.

Her other gift as a novelist is for writing spirited dialogue. The talk of *Belinda* or *Ormonde* is always light, engaging and natural. It is that "modern" talk which goes on from generation to generation—one meets it in Jane Austen; then, after the Regency, it died out, until the modern novel revived it—and which has not been written in, like sub-headings, into the story. Maria Edgeworth owed her gift to her indifference to plot, that great torture-rack of talk in the English novel. Plot was forced on her by her father, the brilliant Major, who suffered from a rather delightful excess of confidence in his own powers; but, like Scott at the beginning of his career, Miss Edgeworth was interested only in sketching the people around her, and that is how the true gift for dialogue arises. Yet she owed something even of this to the Major, for it was he who, determined to out-Rousseau Rousseau, made his daughter write down the dialogue of his twenty-one children in order that it could be examined afterwards in his moral and linguistic laboratory.

Of course, she had the Irish ear for Irish expressiveness. In *Ormonde*, King Corny cries out with the gout:

> "Pray now," said he to Harry who stood beside his bed—"now that I've a moment's ease—did you ever hear of the stoics that the bookmen talk of, and can you tell me what good anyone of them got by making it a point to make no noise when they'd be punished and racked with pains of body or mind? Why I tell you all they got—all they got was no pity—who would give them pity, that did not require it? I could bleed to death in a bath, as well as the best of them, if I chose it; or chew a bullet, if I set my teeth to it, with any man in a regiment—but where's the use? Nature knows best, and she says *roar!*"

In a subtler way, she is as good in her plain passages, notably in her scenes between men and women. She hardly can be said to try a love affair, indeed one might say that she has noticed men and women pursue one another but is not sure why they do so. What she likes best is caprice, misunderstanding, the off-days of married life, flirtation: that side of love which, in short, supplies repartee and comedy, sociability or its opposite. Her people are always being interrupted and, though this shows some incompetence on the novelist's part, it also allows that crisp animation or restlessness which gives her stories their unaffected drift.

There are no interruptions in *Castle Rackrent*. Thady the steward tells the tale in his plain words and with his devious mind, and he rattles off the decline and fall of the riotous Rackrents over three generations, in a hundred pages. Drink, company, debt and recalcitrant foreign wives ruined these roisterers and Thady's own son, turned lawyer, quietly collected the remnant and indirectly made it his own. At the funeral of one Rackrent, the body was nearly seized for debt:

> But the heir who attended the funeral was against that, for fear of consequences, seeing that those villains who came to serve acted under the disguise of the law; so, to be sure, the law must take its course and little gain had the creditors for their pains. First and foremost, they had the curses of the country and Sir Murtagh Rackrent, the new heir, in the next place, on account of this affront to the body refused to pay a shilling of the debts, in which he was countenanced by all best gentlemen of property and others of his acquaintance, Sir Murtagh alleging in all companies that he all along meant to pay his father's debts of honour, but the moment the law was taken from him, there was the end of the honour to be sure. It was whispered (but none but the enemies of the family believe it) that this was all a sham seizure to get quit of the debts, which he had bound himself to pay in honour. It's a long time ago, there's no saying how it was . . .

That is Defoe, but with whiskey added.

Major Edgeworth did not touch *Castle Rackrent*. He is

known to have had a didactic hand in the other works and some have thought he stiffened them. Possibly. Yet his daughter owed her subsequent inspiration to the excitable, inventive, genial mind of the masterful eccentric and amateur. *Castle Rackrent* was the first attempt to present the history of a family over several generations as a subject in itself. It marks a small step in the expansion of the novel. Where the Major's influence is most felt is in the remarkable range of his daughter's work. Ireland is only one of her scenes. English society, Parisian society, are done with the same natural touch. Her work was a triumph for the Major's revolutionary system of free education. Not a patch on Fanny Burney or Jane Austen, no doubt; the minds of father and daughter were too much dispersed by practical and inventive attention to the good, rational life. Scott thought Edgeworthstown a domestic paradise and possibly noted it was an Abbotsford one hundred and fifty years old without the worry and the expense. Abbotsford meant absurdity, obsession, and imagination; Edgeworthstown meant enlightenment. In the last count, the good life does not produce the great novelists.

THE YOUNG GORKY

THE lasting work of Gorky is to be found in the three volumes of autobiography which he wrote between 1913 and 1924 and in the famous portraits of Tolstoy and Andreyev. Most foreign readers have been appalled by the scenes of squalor and gloom which Gorky set down from his life. The opening pages of *Childhood*, are characteristic; Gorky's young and merry father lies dead in the room, the grandmother and the pregnant wife are lamenting, the police are at the door to hurry the funeral, and grief suddenly brings on the wretched mother's labour pains. The child has a terrifying vision of death and birth and there is the inevitable Russian touch of farce: frogs jump on top of the father's coffin as it is lowered into the muddy grave and are buried there. We foresee that Gorky's mother is one of those austere, sensitive, fine women doomed to be destroyed by the brutality and hopelessness of life; and so it turns out, when she takes the child to her father's house. Grandpa has a small dyeworks and is a man of substance. But he has an uncontrollable temper; in his sadistic bouts and partly on pious principle, he beats up the women and children of his family and also his employees. He is surrounded by drunken, quarrelling, vindictive and covetous relatives all whining for his money. Uncle Mike crowns everything by setting the family dyeworks on fire and, in general, one can only say that the cruelty of Nature and the viciousness of the social system are outmatched by the natural animal malice of one human being to another in this book. There *are* scattered moments of goodness and quiet, but the general gloom is relieved by one figure alone: Gorky's grandmother. This captivating old lady is the soul of love and pagan sweetness and a story-teller of genius; there is a strange mixture of mysticism, poetry and stoicism in her nature, and she seems to be a throwback to some earlier, Arcadian phase of the Russian folk. It is because of her influence, as we read on, that our disgust declines. We find we are being seduced by the expressiveness of all Gorky's people, by their self-abandon and by what, later on, Gorky is to call their capacity for turning their sorrows into carnival. Fatalism does not always degrade: it often enlarges.

Gorky does not snarl; he neither maunders nor does he coarsely glut a secret appetite. He is totally free of that hysterical connivance which we get from Zola; he is never prolonging a private orgy. He is not a sensationalist wallowing in the sins of society; nor is he a smug social realist congratulating himself, like some Victorian reformer, that he at any rate has the right social and political views. We are elated because in these books Gorky has the heroic eye, a sort of giant-creating eye; because he has the strongest compassion, and practises an almost saintly exclusion of himself from his own life. What matters to him is the strange spectacle of humanity. The boy grows, but the world grows too; everything is in physical movement. Gorky has a memory, we say, that allows the world to have existed to the full, without first having to ask a tacit moral or intellectual permission from himself. He has his standards, of course, he has his fastidiousness and there *is* a judgment, but none of these distorts his emotions or robs his extraordinary eye of its pity and its liberty.

Some critics have pointed out that Gorky's realism is a revolt against the puritanism of earlier Russian writers; if this is so, we notice that it takes a puritan to revolt, though many puritans relapse instead and go to seed. Gorky retains the puritan core, the puritan energy and tenacity; he is moved by what he mixes in with—the orgy at Petrovsky's in *My Universities*, for example—he is marked by it, yet he retains his integrity and he is not corrupted. An interesting reflection on his pessimism is made by Mirsky in his *History of Russian Literature*.

> Gorky [he says] is not a pessimist and if he is, his pessimism has nothing to do with his representation of Russian life, but rather with the chaotic state of his philosophical views, which he has never succeeded in making serve his optimism, in spite of all his efforts in that direction. As it is Gorky's autobiographical series represents the world as ugly but not unrelieved—the redeeming points which may and must save humanity, are enlightenment, beauty and sympathy.

This is the optimism native to all artists which is always more important than what they *think* they believe and is frequently at complete variance with it. In the course of his sometimes portentous self-education, Gorky was never able to tame his extraordinary eye. It remained autonomous and unweakened, a kind of person in itself like one of those boys that lead the blind. Indeed that is how Gorky often seems to us: a powerful, blind man being led by a voracious, all-seeing child.

To an astonishing extent all Russian literature is led blindly on by the inconsequence of the eye. Russian fantasy, the effect of the naïve and childish, the sudden dislocations which make the Russian novel so loose and life-like, above all the sense of the grotesque, owe everything to it. To some extent this use of the eye—and also the habit of describing violently contradictory feelings almost in the same breath—have stereotyped Russian literature for the foreign reader who is, perforce, unable to see differences of style. But one has only to compare Tolstoy's superb use of the eye with Gorky's to see there *are* differences and that this is not a national manner alone. Tolstoy watches life unblinkingly, like some subtle, impartial animal whose many faceted lenses reflect all without effort. He lies still and natural life is imprinted on him line by line. Gorky, on the other hand, is like a hundred-eyed man who goes aggressively into life catching detail at every blink and who amazes us by forgetting nothing. Where he looks something is always happening. If a foolish soldier has turned to face his tormentors, Gorky sees him tuck his shirt in; if half a dozen chickens are being chased on a boat, he will see three fly overboard; he will remember how many times his grandmother told him to get from under her feet when the dyeworks caught fire, and afterwards see her blow on her scorched fingers as she talks; he will remember thousands of faces and gestures, every change of mood, every word spoken in his grandpa's tormented family, in the shops, ships and sheds where he worked, or on the roads where he tramped. The seeing and hearing are consuming. If the whole is invented memory, it is invented down to the most casual acts and finest shades and in a manner seemingly effortless. As far as I can define it the art seems to lie in combining contrasting things; in his accounts of people he first describes their appearance or their life from the outside and then catches something unexpected which reveals a part of the inner life that is bubbling away inside them. This is what human beings look like (he seems to say)—violent, vindictive, malicious, foolish, innocent, unfortunate, rascally or good—but what is on their minds all day, how do they get through the hours? So much fighting, scheming, quarrelling, hoping, suffering—but what is deposited by it all for their empty moments, what is their particular form of the human bewilderment? So, for example, when the boy is left with the temper of his uncontrollable grandfather:

> I lost all interest in grandpa's talk which grew duller, more nagging, more self-pitying, day by day. It had practically become a habit with him to quarrel with grandma

> and forbid her the house, and then she stayed at Uncle Mike's or Uncle Jake's. Once she was away for a number of days and grandpa cooked for us. He burned his fingers, yelled, cursed, smashed dishes; and he became noticeably gluttonous. Coming to my little hut, now and then, he would take his ease on my turf bench and, after watching me for a time would suddenly ask: "Why so quiet?"
>
> "Because I prefer it. Why?"
>
> And that would precipitate a lecture. "We're not upper crust. No one bothers about our education. We have to learn by ourselves. For them books are written and schools are built; but no time is thrown away on us. We have to get along by ourselves." And he lapsed into a preoccupied silence; he made me feel uncomfortable and tense, as he sat there inert and oblivious.

The next moment the pious, diddling old savage is turning his old wife out of the house, saying that he has fed her long enough. But whereas a pitiless satirist like Shchedrin portrayed such a man in the storming and whining hypocrite Iudushka, Gorky sees people as victims of forces they do not understand and not as souls wicked in themselves. Grandpa is horrible, but he is also absurd, touching and not without a queer, half-frightened dignity.

Gorky's judgments are instinctive, not intellectual. He is torn between compassion and an aggressive resentment, himself as contradictory as the characters he draws. As he reflects upon the murderous quarrels in the home where he was brought up, he says:

> In time I came to understand that out of the misery and murk of their lives the Russian people had learned to make sorrow a diversion, to play with it like a child's toy; seldom are they diffident about showing their unhappiness. And so through the tedious weekdays, they make a carnival of grief; a fire is entertainment, and on a vacant face a bruise becomes an adornment.

A carnival, these three volumes of autobiography are, a carnival that wanders all over the Russia that existed before the beginning of this century, steadied here and there by one or two serious people of goodwill and illuminated by the gracious old figure of the grandmother, the pagan saint and story-teller. This old woman is beaten from time to time, like everyone else in the book, but she takes that with a guileless and humble laugh, goes on with her stories and her simple pantheism. She has the civilisation and humanity of a poet. What Gorky understood as an artist he must have learned from her. She chanted her tales:

> When she had finished I begged for another, and this is an example of what I got. "Now an old goblin lives in the stove. Once he ran a splinter into his paw. As he rocked back and forth with the pain, he whined 'I can't bear it, little mice, it hurts so much.' "
>
> And she lifted her own foot in her hands and rocked it comically, screwing up her face as if she actually felt the pain.
>
> The bearded, good-natured sailors would listen, too, and applauding the stories would urge: "Give us another, grandma." And in reward they would invite us to supper with them. There they plied her with vodka and me with watermelon. This was done in secret, for there was a man patrolling the boat, dressed like an official, who forbade the eating of fruit, confiscating whatever he found and throwing it overboard. Everybody kept out of the way of this man who, besides, was perpetually drunk.

The story and Gorky's epilogue have the same turn of inconsequence, the same immediate candour and acceptance of life.

Gorky is a writer strong as cheese and raw as onion. It is strange to think of him reading Fielding and praising the trim English as the originators and masters of realism, for his vision is heroic. He had a primitive directness of apprehension, a sensibility unspoiled by civilisation. That he was idolised by the people was just; like them he was growing; like them he drew his imaginative forces from the past. He was really a life rather than a novelist, a learned and circumspect vagrant who became, for one period, as Mirsky says, the only alternative government in Russia. What he lived and saw, not what he constructed, contained his importance. Often intellectually indigestible as a writer he is always a blind, moving force.

NEW YORK, 1900

A NOVEL by Mrs Wharton in her best period is a correcting experience, a pain when the correction seems to be directed at ourselves, a pleasure when it is being handed out to other people. She is—so many of the important women novelists have been this—a mother-figure, determined, pragmatic, critical and alarming. How inevitable not to come up to her moral, intellectual, above all her social standards. Once we get out of the room where we have been sitting alone with the formidable lady, we foresee that we shall break out or go downhill once more. We know she is no fool; she can startle us by her range of observation; but we shall suspect that what she calls discipline is really first cousin to puritanism and fear, and that what she calls the Eumenides are really projections of the aunts who run the conventions and man the barricades of the taboos. The acerbity of a novelist, like Mrs Wharton is *mondain* before it is intellectual; it denotes a positive pleasure in the fact that worldly error has to be heavily paid for spiritually. Her sense of tragedy is linked to a terrifying sense of propriety. It is steely and has the hard efficiency of the property market into which she was born. When, in *The House of Mirth*, Lily Bart is told that she will have to choose between the values of the smart set in New York and the "republic of the spirit", we are not absolutely convinced that this republic is not a new kind of puritan snobbery. The men who belong to this republic signally fail to rush the women off their feet into this excellent world, and Mrs Wharton is drily aware of their failure. In its first decades the rise of American Big Business created an upper class whose sensitive men cut themselves off from a crude society that shocked them and which was dominated by women. She noted this in her autobiography and it is plain in all her books. Her own interesting situation is that there is an emotional force held back in her, which resents the things her mind approves of and it is this dilemma that gives her mind its cutting edge—at any rate in the books she wrote before she found personal happiness. That happiness, it now seems, dulled her talent.

There is, of course, more than all this to Mrs Wharton, both as person and novelist. She elaborated the balance sheet of renunciation and became the accountant-historian of a rich society, and nothing passed her merciless eye. She wrote best when the pressure had been hardest to bear, even though that pressure may have frozen the imaginative and enhanced the critical character of her talent. Her prose has a presentable cold pomp: "The cushioned chairs, disposed expectantly under the wide awning, showed no signs of recent occupancy." Under great bitterness and frustration we have learned to expect outbursts of sentimentality—as a far greater writer, like Mauriac, has shown us—and when she drags the Eumenides into three or four melodramatic pages of her best novel, *The House of Mirth*, we are embarrassed. But it is exceptional for her control to go. Her study of rich New York in the early 1900's in that book will pass for smart sets anywhere and at any time, for even in our day, when most conventions have gone, when people no longer behave like "deaf mutes in an asylum", the cheerless figure of the socialite remains. The smart set is the quintessential dust bowl. In a later comment on this novel Mrs Wharton wrote "that a frivolous society can acquire dramatic significance only through what its frivolity destroys. Its tragic implication lies in its power of debasing people and ideals." The idea is Jamesian and if the execution of it lacks the poetry, the heightened recitative of Henry James, we do get from Mrs Wharton the hard, unpitying moralist who will forgive but not forget, and the derisive critic of social architecture.

Indignation about the sins of another social class is, of course, easy money, and does not, of itself, get a novelist very far. One slightly suspects that Mrs Wharton did not like new people getting rich. But she did examine her subject with scientific efficiency, and in Lily Bart she created the most rewarding kind of socialite: one who was morally a cut above the rest of her circle, but who had been fatally conditioned from the first. Lily Bart is a beautiful and very intelligent girl, delightful company and really too clever for any of the men her society was likely to offer. On the lowest level, she is hopeless about money, about pushing her way in first, about intrigue, about using people, about the main chance. Her own view is that she behaves as she does, because she has no money. It is Becky Sharp's cry: virtue on five thousand a year. But this is only half her case. She is a superb artist in the business of being in the swim, a brilliant contriver of success; she has a wonderful sense of timing—when to be in the spotlight and when not. Her startling weakness is that she sows but she does not reap. At the last moment she is wrecked by the sudden boredom and carelessness of the very clever. On the day of victory she oversleeps. Her self-confidence is such that she does not bother to play her ace; and she imagines her gift for dispensing with success at the last minute will make her impervious to her enemies. It does not. Selden, who wants to marry her, imagines that her last-minute failures are signs of grace, impulses from the unconscious. They make her very likeable, but they must be considered as opportunities for further displays of courage and sangfroid rather than happy, non-social back-slidings into "the republic of the spirit". Her courage is half vanity. So low are the standards of her set that she is encouraged thereby to mistake thrilled nerve for an access of intelligence:

> She . . . listened to Ned Silverton reading Theocritus by moonlight, as the yacht rounded the Sicilian promontories, with a thrill of the nerves that confirmed her belief in her intellectual superiority.

Theocritus is, in short, the right poet, at the right moment, among the right people, at the height of the season. A venial folly; after all, are we quite sure that the enlightened Selden is any better for cutting himself off from the life of his country and reading La Bruyère?

Lily Bart has the beauty and vanity which George Eliot thought so wicked in women, but Lily's attractions are energy, an occasional capacity for honesty and innocence. She is not ashamed of her cunning in getting money out of a married man like Gus Trenor, for she has used her brains; what really shocks her is the price demanded. Her match is Rosedale, the rich rising Jew who reads her character perfectly, who puts his price up as hers goes down and, in the end, out of sheer admiration for her abilities, is willing to behave disinterestedly. But he is defeated by her gift for last-minute failure: she refuses to silence the women who have ruined her. Pride or a sense of virtue? Neither, I think —and here Mrs Wharton is very penetrating: those who believe in their star believe also in despair. Lily Bart is a gambler. One enjoys her as one enjoys the electric shocks of roulette, as one enjoys the incorrigible and the plunger. And one enjoys her also because Mrs Wharton turns her inside out:

> Moral complications existed for her only in the environment that had produced them: she did not mean to slight or ignore them, but they lost their reality when they changed their background.

Or, when it is a matter of getting a financial "tip" out of Trenor:

> She was always scrupulous about keeping up appearances to herself. Her personal fastidiousness had a moral equivalent and when she made a tour of inspection in her own mind there were certain closed doors she did not open.

The only element missing from Lily Bart's character is her obvious sexual coldness to which, when the novel was written, Mrs Wharton could hardly have referred even if—to suppose the impossible—she had desired to do so.

New York's social scene is expertly set down in *The House of Mirth* with an anthropologist's thoroughness and the novel is remarkable for its skilful visits from one smart set to the smart set on the stair below. These tours are conducted with all Mrs Wharton's superlative snobbery.

> Mrs Bry, to Mrs Fisher's despair had not progressed beyond the point of weighing her social advantages in public.

There was smart hotel society:

> Through this atmosphere of torrid splendour moved wan beings as richly upholstered as the furniture, beings without definite pursuits or permanent relations, who drifted on a languid tide of curiosity from restaurant to concert hall, from palm-garden to music-room.

Here reigned Mrs Hatch, the simple lady who, surrounded by beauty specialists, wished to soar socially; the Bovary of the gossip columns, who wanted to do what was "nice" and to be taught how to be "lovely".

Mrs Wharton hated the smart set she had been brought up in and she is good in this novel no doubt because she is anatomising the monster whose stupidities and provincialities might have crushed her. But the making of her as a novelist is her power to create incident and to conduct great scenes.

Strangely enough her ironical power and gift of surprise often recall those of an utterly different novelist—Thomas Hardy. She has—usually under iron control—a persistent sense of fate, a skill in entangling her characters before striking them down. The scene at Gus Trenor's when this magnate turns nasty and looks like going to the point of sexual assault is wonderfully handled and Lily is marvellous in it; every cliché in this well-known situation is avoided, every truth in it discerned and the end is perfect. And Bertha Dorset's revenge on Lily: that is as brilliant a *volte-face* and surprise as one can remember in any plot in social comedy. Mrs Wharton did not touch these heights afterwards, though even in her weaker novels, there is the same astringency, the same readiness of invention.

Again and again we find that novelists who have attacked the conventions because they stultify the spirit, who attack the group for its cruelty to individuals, will end by pointing out the virtues of submission. Mrs Wharton may have hated old New York, but she hated the new New York even more. She disliked the prison of silent hypocrisy, but she drew in her skirts when candour came in. Especially after her long life, *en grande luxe*, in Europe. What indignation denounces creeps back in the name of sentiment. *The Age of Innocence* shows a man giving in, loyally marrying the conventional girl he does not love, throwing over the Europeanised woman who is his natural equal. It is the surrender to the established bourgeois standard. No great harms come of it; only dullness and disappointment. The sweet young girl he was engaged to was slyer than he thought. She became like her mother-in-law to whose face "a lifelong mastery over trifles had given factitious authority". Perhaps, after all, her husband reflects, that old New York which would not "know" a divorced woman, was rather charming and quite right. Better renunciation than a hole-in-corner affair. Mrs Wharton always believed in the sterner condition; but her brain resented it. Not even snobbery and respect for "factitious authority" could get her into the Catholic Church at the end of her life. The old Puritan worldling stood out firmly for patching, for facing unpleasantness, making the second best of things, refusing accommodations. Worry, culture and character were the thing. One imagines God wondering if he dared leave a card. The strange thing is that we mistrust her at once when, late in life, she becomes benign.

A VIENNESE

ROBERT MUSIL'S *The Man Without Qualities* is an immense unfinished novel, which this Czech-Austrian began writing in the 'twenties and was still working on when he died an exile in Geneva in 1942. It is a wonderful and prolonged firework display, a well-peopled comedy of ideas, on the one hand; on the other, an infiltration into the base areas of what we call "the contemporary predicament". There is the pleasure of a cleverness which is not stupid about life: "Even mistrust of oneself and one's destiny here assumed the character of profound self-certainty," Musil wrote—not altogether ironically—of the Austrian character and these words suggest the conflict which keeps the book going at its cracking speed. Of course, Musil's kind of egoism had a long run in the first twenty years of the century and he has been—the translators tell us—written down by the standard German literary histories. Musil's tongue does indeed run away with him; but it is stupid to denigrate him. Proust and Joyce, with whom he has been exaggeratedly compared, approached the self by way of the aesthetic imagination; Musil reconstructs egos intellectually. What ideas do our sensations suggest? What processes are we involved in? If Musil has come to us regrettably late, if he sticks for his subject matter to the old pre-1914 Vienna and has some of that period flavour, he is not stranded there. The revival of Henry James has taught us that writers who live passively within history may be more deeply aware of what is really going on than those who turn up in every spot where the news is breaking.

The nearest parallel to Musil is not Proust but Italo Svevo

in *The Confessions of Zeno.* Musil is very much an intellectual of that strain. The two writers represent opposite sides of the same Viennese school. They are restless, headlong psychologists and sceptical talkers, to some extent café writers. Like Zeno, the Ulrich of *The Man Without Qualities* is a gifted and self-consuming man. He burns up his experience. But whereas Zeno is a hypochondriac, a man of endless self-doubt, the clown of the imagination and the heart, whose great comic effect is obtained by the pursuit of folly with passionate seriousness, Ulrich is a healthy, athletic extroverted and worldly character whose inquiring brain captivates and disturbs men of action. He is a mind before he is a sensibility. He has only to appear for others to behave absurdly; his irony muddles them; his perception alarms. Musil's achievement is to make this formidable character tolerable and engaging. Ulrich is endlessly, perhaps pitilessly patient; he has learned that humility of the intellect which comes of continuous use and which is necessary to those who look into other people for what may be useful to their own imaginative and intellectual search. Like Zeno he can never resist a theory; but whereas Zeno's love for other people is really a kind of remorse for having had so many ideas about himself, the love of Ulrich is a feeling of gratitude to others for suggesting so many ideas that he has been free of them personally. His attraction and power come from an imagination which transposes. Here is a comment on one of his comic characters, a cabaret singer, a Juno of refinement who has a passion for eating. After a good meal she would feel obliged to repay her lover:

> She would stand up and tranquilly, but full throatedly, lift up her voice in song. For her protector such evenings were like pages torn out of an album, animated by all sorts of inspirations and ideas, but mummified, as everything becomes when it is torn out of its context, loaded with the

> tyrannical spell of all that will now remain eternally the way it is, the thing that is the uncanny fascination of *tableaux vivants* when it is as though life had suddenly been given a sleeping draught; and now there it stands, rigid, perfectly correlated within it itself, clearly outlined in its immense futility against the background of the world.

One can see, after this, why Musil has been compared with Proust—though, if the translation is to be relied upon, he does not write as well—yet, where Proust seeks to crystallise a past, Musil is always pushing through that strange undergrowth to find out, if possible, where he is, where life is tending, and what is the explanation. His book is a crab-wise search for a future, for what has not yet been given the sleeping draught.

In the first half of Part One of the novel the time and scene are the Vienna of the Austrian Empire. The main episodes are Ulrich's love affairs with the guzzling singer and with a rueful nymphomaniac; his friendship with a gifted but unstable girl and with a superb bourgeois lady, notorious for mind, whom he calls Diotima, and who goes in for the True, the Good, the Beautiful on the grand scale. Diotima is a monument, an outsize schoolgirl. But the larger themes are political and social. Before long we have, by brilliant implication, an amusing but moving picture of a complete society whose intentions become nobler the nearer it is to destruction. Nobler and more absurd. For Musil has invented a wonderful farce called the Collateral Campaign. This vague political movement is meant somehow and simultaneously to celebrate the Emperor's birthday, boost Austrian culture—with a meaning glance at the Germans—preserve the stagnant existing order and yet arise spontaneously from the hearts of the common people and bring new spiritual life to the greatest minds desiccated by scepticism, intellectualism, etc. In short it is an all-purpose piece of uplift which is touchingly sincere and hopelessly muddled. It is very fond of the word "true"—not patriotism but "true" patriotism, not values but "true" values. The comic beauty of the Collateral Campaign is that it can never settle on its precise form; it swells into committees, exhausts all the clichés, and turns into its opposite: a movement for chauvinism and rearmament. Really it is a midwife of Fascism. Nothing is more certain of comic reward than Musil's sympathy. It is tender and deadly.

The people of the Collateral Campaign are "good". They are responsible. They represent "the best elements". They can choose. They choose ridiculously. But what of the bad, the irresponsible who cannot choose—a man like the homicidal maniac Moosbrugger who may or may not be executed? (He wants to be executed because he has an almost pettifogging regard for the law.) The Moosbrugger case puts its shadow on all the characters in the book and one of Musil's feats as a novelist is to show us exactly how Moosbrugger seeps into every mind in some way or other. If society is tending towards progress what is it going to do about this Caliban? Ulrich reflects; "If mankind could dream collectively it would dream Moosbrugger." If we do not know by what absolute standards to settle the Moosbrugger case, then a great social catastrophe is inevitable. Writing in the 'twenties Musil could hardly have been more prophetic.

There is an interesting account of Musil's life in the very good introduction to the Wilkins and Kaiser translation of his novel. He came, we are told, of a gifted family. He was educated for the Army, fought in the 1914 war, became a civil engineer, a distinguished inventor, a mathematician, a psychologist, and was about to teach philosophy at Munich before he turned to writing. Musil brought to his writing not only the capacity for seeing but also the habit of hypothesis. Ulrich is, in many ways, Musil translated. In his several attempts to define what he means by "the man without qualities", he notes,

> He will perform actions that mean something different to him from what they mean to others, but is reassured about everything as soon as it can be summed up in an extraordinary idea.

Or again, the translators give us these lines from the page he was adding to the last volume of his novel on the day he died:

> Of course it was clear to him that the two kinds of human being . . . could mean nothing else than a man without qualities and, in contrast, the man with all the qualities that anyone could manage to display. And the one might be called a nihilist, dreaming of God's dreams—in contrast to the activist who is, however, with his impatient way of acting, a kind of God's dreamer too, and anything but a realist, who goes about being worldly clear and worldly active.

Consciousness was Musil's real subject, not the "stream" but the architecture, the process of building, stylising and demolishing that goes on in the mind. How does an idea like the Collateral Campaign grow in various minds? How, sensuously, does it breed? At what point does sensation become idea? How does reality look after that intoxication? These things bring out Musil's alacrity and focusing power as a novelist; for though he never stops talking he always enacts what he sees. He has a poetic yet practical ability for showing an idea coming to someone—a slow-minded and simple aristocrat, a blackamoor servant, a woman beginning to feel indignation and remorse in love, any transition in fact from one state of consciousness to another. He has the merit of loving people for their essence. There is, to take one example, a striking study of that special bourgeois protégé, the failed artist who takes to blaming his failure on the collapse of culture. From a hero he has turned into a petty domestic tyrant and rules his wife, who has ceased to love him, by making her play duets on the piano. Their marriage is sustained by a neurotic frenzy of piano-playing:

> The next moment Clarisse and Walter shot away like two railway engines racing side by side. The music that they were playing came flying towards their eyes like the glittering rails, then vanished under the thundering engine and spread out behind them, as a chiming, resonant, miraculously permanent landscape. . . . Precise to a fraction of a second, gaiety, sadness, anger, fear, love and hatred, longing and weariness went flying through Walter and Clarisse. It was a union like in a great panic. But it was not the same mindless, overwhelming force that life has. . . .

The more music sublimely unites them, the more they are separated in life, each thinking his way away from the other. Walter, the rejected husband, fearing failure and impotence, begins to slip into thoughts comfortably too large for him, and ends by playing Wagner for erotic reassurance. Here he begins to strike wrong notes. Clarisse's mind jumps from image to image and to questions becoming more and more savage: does civilised life yearn for brutality? Does peacefulness call for cruelty? For there is an empty room in Clarisse where "something tore at the chains". At the end of this volume we get a glimpse of that empty room.

In making raids like this into Musil's novel one risks making it sound thin or melodramatic in the heavy Central European way; a pound of realism to a ton of essay-writing. He is, on the contrary, subtle, light, liquid, serious. He is, no doubt, a bit over-fond of himself, perhaps a bit too tolerant to the "I" who is never brought up against anything stronger than itself; a bit too much on the spot, especially in the love affairs. What the novel does show is that the habit of intellectual analysis is not stultifying to drama, movement or invention, but enhances them. It is a delightful insight that a movement like the Collateral Campaign, which has no distinctive idea, will inevitably attract all those people in the Austrian Empire who have only one idea; it is perfect that Ulrich shall be put in charge of sorting out these cranks. His theories, the whole apparatus of the book, are the forgiveness of the artist, not the examination papers of the master. Consciousness is, for him, a pardonable folly. Some critics have discerned what they believe to be a mythological foundation to this novel, in the manner of *Ulysses*; the density, suggestiveness and range could support the view. For it is cunningly engineered. The second volume of *The Man Without Qualities* sustains the impression of a major writer of comedy in the Viennese manner, and of an original imagination.

A French friend of Musil's, M. Bernard Guillemin, suggests that what Musil meant by "a man without Qualities" (*Mann ohne Eigenschaften*), was "a man completely disengaged and uncommitted or a man in quest of non-accidental attributes and responsibilities self-chosen—the German counterpart of Gide's '*homme disponible*' though there is nothing of Gide in Musil's work". In the later volumes, it is said to have worried Musil himself, that a character as disengaged as Ulrich is, will eventually become isolated and by-passed by life. The sense of adventure which exhilarates the early volumes, becomes paralysed in the later ones, where the intellectually liberated man is not able to take the next step into "right action". It is significant that Musil's novel was never finished. He had spun a brilliant web of perceptions round himself and was imprisoned by them.

In this second volume, the absurd Collateral Campaign is still going on in Austria, Diotima, the lofty-minded Egeria, who runs the social side, discovers the "soul" just as she is getting tired of her husband, a high government official. She has risen out of the middle classes into aristocratic society, and she plants this idea of the soul in an international financier and arms manufacturer, a German called Arnheim. There are Generals who come in because "the Army must keep an eye on things"; Diotima's social rivals appear to keep an eye on her, and so on. There is a wonderfully complete picture of a society at the edge of the precipice of 1914. The novelist's comic sense of character is speculative, and is strengthened by his penetration into the kinds of consciousness current at the time, into how private ideas become public, and public ideas affect the emotions of private life.

In the meantime, the Moosbrugger case—Moosbrugger is the homicidal sex maniac awaiting execution—underlies the social picture and makes its own disturbing footnotes. What about the law's attitude to insanity in murder; what about violence in the state, in personal life? At the most unexpected moments, Moosbrugger—who is merely a name in the papers to most of the characters—raises his idiot head and poses his devastating questions. "Ordinary life," Ulrich concludes, "is an intermediate state made up of all our possible crimes." So Musil dresses a platitude in epigrammatic form; he becomes rather free with epigrams; but his gift is to enact epigrams imaginatively.

In this volume the analysis of character is done at much greater length than in the introductory volume and so there is more discussion and less action. Of the portraits, Arnheim's and the absurd yet subtle General's are the most impressive, but we must not omit the girl Gerda and her lover who are moving towards an early form of Fascism. Musil's Arnheim is by far the most cogent and exhaustive study of a millionaire magnate's mind that I have ever read. The irony is exact and continuous. Arnheim, for example, had "the gift of being a paragon":

> Through his understanding of this delicate interlocking of all forms of life, which only the blind arrogance of the ideologist can forget, Arnheim came to see the prince of commerce as the synthesis of revolution and permanence, of armed power and bourgeois civilisation, of reasoned audacity and honest to goodness knowledge, but essentially as a symbolic prefiguration of the kind of democracy that was about to come into existence . . . he hoped to meet the new age half-way.

Under the influence of his love for Diotima, Arnheim seeks to bring about the "fusion of interests between Business and the Soul". His craving for power leads him to writing books: "with positively spectral prolixity" his pen began to pour out reflections on "the need of this fusion" and "it is equally certain that his ambition to master all there was to be known . . . found in the soul a means of devaluing everything that his intellect could not master". Arnheim is morally devastated by his love for Diotima, for she is monumentally high-minded; and Musil has the pleasure of showing us a sumptuous, high-minded *femme du monde* reduced to the frantic condition of a woman forced to the bed of a testy, cynical husband, and a magnate paradoxically reverting to his native instincts the more his "soul" is elevated. All roads leave from the soul, Musil reflects, but none lead back to it: Arnheim is no more than a magnate after all and, once Diotima can be his, he falls back on the old maxim that in love, as in business, one had better spend only the interest, not the capital. Arnheim's character reminds one of Walter Bagehot's dictum that a kind of intellectual twilight, with all its vagueness, is necessary to the man of business and, towards the end of this volume, Musil reveals what Arnheim is really after in the ideological mists of the Collateral Campaign and the higher life of Diotima: he is after control of the Galician oilfields.

Ulrich, the man without qualities, is the natural enemy of Arnheim; his natural foil is the comic General. An air of unworldliness in civilian life is an obligatory mask of the military profession; all "a poor soldier man" may permit himself to point out is that, if the military have a virtue, it is their sense of order. There is a farcical scene of discussion when this soldier describes his visit to the National Library where he approaches the whole task of improving his mind in the spirit of the strategist. The General is a wit in his way. Even after a carefully worked-out campaign of reading, in which he allows for substantial casualties, he discovers it will still take him 10,000 years to read what is necessary. "There must be something wrong about that," he says, raising his glass of brandy.

Musil writes with the heightened sensibility of a man in love; that is to say, under the influence of the unrest of seeking a harmony and completion in things. The Collateral Campaign itself is a kind of communal love affair. In the description of love affairs and especially in the portraits of women in love, Musil is truly original; in managing scenes of physical love, he has not been approached by any writer of the last fifty years. What has been missing, in those accounts, has been Musil's transcendent subject: the sense of the changing architecture of consciousness. He brings the effect of the imagination into the fears and desires of these women, their sense of living out an idea which may indeed well be a love fantasy about quite a different lover from the one in whose bed they lie. He is sensitive to the power of "erotic distraction". Of Rachel, the maid who goes to bed with a fellow servant because she has been stirred by the touch of a guest's hand, he writes:

> The object of this yearning was actually Ulrich, and Solimon was cast in the role of the man whom one does

> not love and to whom one will nevertheless abandon oneself—a point on which Rachel was in no sort of doubt whatsoever. For the fact that she was not allowed to be with him, that for some time past they had hardly ever spoken to each other except in a whisper, and that the displeasure of those in authority over them had descended upon them both, had much the effect on her as a night full of uncertainty, uncanny happenings, and sighs has on anyone in love; it all concentrated her smouldering fancies like a burning glass, the beam of which is felt less as an agreeable warmth than as something one will not be able to stand much longer.

The high-minded love affair, the violently neurotic, the absurd one, the desperate affair carried on against the will, the one crossed by other lives; from all these Musil extracts the essence with dignity and gaiety, the comi-tragedy of human loss and incompleteness. The history of love is the history of absence, of arrival and departure. He is able to do what no contemporary ever does: to move from the imaginative and emotional to the physical without change of voice; even the naked fight on the bed or the brazen or terrified undressings are not marred by the worst fault of our erotic realism: its unconscious grotesque. The tenderness, subtlety and disinterestedness of Musil's intelligence enable him to do this; and the almost conversational style. Critics tell us that, whatever the awkwardness of translation may be, he has in German a style that is as lucid as that of Anatole France and less florid than Proust's. One cannot judge this, though the translation of the second volume seems to me an improvement on the first. (The whole difficulty has been to avoid translating German abstractions into the kind of technical or administrative super-jargon which these become in English.) Musil is an addiction. The most irrelevant criticism made of him by some Germans and Austrians is that his kind of café sensibility is out of date.

It may certainly be familiar in Schnitzler and Svevo, but Musil's whole scheme prophetically describes the bureaucratic condition of our world, and what can only be called the awful, deadly serious and self-deceptive love affair of one committee for another. And he detects the violence underneath it all. In only one sense is he out of date: he can conceive of a future, of civilised consciousness flowing on and not turning back sick and doomed upon itself.

QUIXOTE'S TRANSLATORS

DON QUIXOTE has been called the novel that killed a country by knocking the heart out of it and extinguishing its belief in itself for ever. The argument might really be the other way on. *Don Quixote* was written by the poor soldier and broken tax-collector with the hand maimed in his country's battles because the Spanish dream of Christian chivalry and total power had passed the crisis of success. The price of an illusion was already being paid and Cervantes marked it down. When Don Quixote recovered his sanity, his soul lost its forces, and he died. What must strike the foreign reader is the difference between the book as it appears to Spaniards and as it appears to the world outside of Spain. The difference is that in Spain *Don Quixote* had a basis in contemporary fact; outside Spain it is morality, metaphysics, fable. The romances of chivalry were read during the Counter-Reformation and specifically moved two of the Spanish saints to action—St Teresa and St Ignatius de Loyola. Longing for the freedom of a man as her brothers went off to the New World, St Teresa read these books with excitement, and Loyola's famous vigil at Manresa was made consciously in imitation of Amadis, and might be a chapter of *Don Quixote*.

Outside Spain, the novel began a new life in countries where the idea of chivalry had no tradition of national awakening and power, where the tragic core was missing. To the English and French translators who got to work a few years after the book was published, *Don Quixote* was simply the greatest of the picaresque novels, indeed the only great one in a genre which elsewhere kept strictly to exaggeration, meaninglessness and popular anarchy. The book became farce—though the contemporary Shelton sins far less than Motteux who translated the book at the beginning of the eighteenth century—a string of adventures and scenes of horseplay tied up with ironical conversations about the noble disadvantages of idealism and its conflict with proverbial self-interest. If we turn to the English novelists who, in the early eighteenth century, were deeply influenced by the tale, we can see how they altered the characters of Don Quixote and Sancho to suit the new middle-class morality. Don Quixote, especially, the violent and subtle madman with his visions of the lost Golden Age, becomes in England a mere eccentric, an unaccountable squire, a hilarious Scot in Smollett, an unworldly but rough-and-tumble clergyman in Fielding. Figures like Parson Adams are misfits, cranks, clowns, often enlightened but always simple and without authority; whereas Don Quixote's mind is darkened and dignified by the counsels of his madness. He has the endless resource of the neurotic; he has pride and the habits of pride and command. In England, the ingenious gentleman is opposed by the worthy forces of self-interest, so much admired in Cheapside. The question is practical: idealism or realism? The answer always sentimental: failure is lovable and what is lovable is commercial. These imitators in the sensible eighteenth century delight in freaks because they love individuality; but they do not enter, as Cervantes in his great mercy did, into that universal region of the human spirit where the imagination reigns like an ungovernable and fretful exile in a court of shadows.

The late Samuel Putnam translated *Don Quixote* and three of the *Exemplary Novels*. They were published in handsome volumes printed on a fine large page—a great advantage—and contain a critical account of many earlier translations and a very large collection of valuable notes; altogether a scholarly piece of work by an American amateur. He had translated a good deal of Brazilian literature. Mr. Putnam believed *Don Quixote* to be one of the dying classics and thought an accurate and contemporary translation might revive it. Compared with Shelton, the abominated Motteux—the one guessed and the other added colour—with Ormsby, Jervas and even the Penguin done efficaciously (especially in the dialogue) by J. M. Cohen, Putnam's translation is toned down. This means that the fine shading of the irony of Cervantes becomes clear and Mr Putnam has taken great trouble with the difficult proverbs. A few contemporary colloquialisms, mainly American, surprise but do not seem out of place; there is often a mildness in Mr Putnam which leads him to choose a weak word or phrase where the Castilian is strong, terse and concrete; and in straining after accuracy he has missed sometimes the note of repartee or satirical echo in the conversations of Don Quixote and Sancho. In the scene at the inn with Maritornes and the muleteer, and in the chapter following, Motteux, Jervas and Cohen—to take only three—are superior in vigour to Mr Putnam, whose colloquial phrases have a cityfied smoothness from easy over-use. To give an example: Don Quixote is about to reveal that the daughter of the supposed Castilian had come to him in the night, but stops to make Sancho swear that he will tell no one about this until after the Knight is dead, for he will not allow anyone's honour to be damaged. Sancho replies, without tact, that he swears, but hopes that he will be free to reveal the secret tomorrow, on the grounds that: "It's just that I am opposed to keeping things too long—I don't like them to spoil on my hands."

Both Motteux and Cohen stick closer to the more vigorous original image. The Spanish word is "go mouldy" or even "rot", and not "spoil". Literally "go mouldy on me". In the earlier chapter one can catch Motteux adding direct, eighteenth-century animal coarseness where Cervantes is not coarse at all; in fact, *Don Quixote* is unique in picaresque literature in its virtual freedom from obscenity, except in some of the oaths. When Maritornes rushes to Sancho's bed to hide there from her angry master, Motteux writes:

> The wench . . . fled for shelter to Sancho's sty, where he lay snoring to some tune; there she pigged in and lay snug as an egg.

This is picturesque, but it has arisen from the mistranslation of two words in the text. Possibly it is an improvement on Cervantes who wrote merely that "she went to Sancho's bed and curled up in a ball". Mr Putnam's pedantry spoils his accuracy here for, instead of "ball", he writes, "ball of yarn". The objection to Motteux is that in making Cervantes picturesque and giving him Saxon robustness, he endangers the elegance and the finely drawn out subtleties of the original. Motteux was half-way to Smollett, which is a long way from Cervantes. The picturesque and pungent in Cervantes lie wholly in Sancho's proverbs, where Mr Putnam excels. When Doña Rodriguez says that she can see "the advantage which a maiden duenna has over a widow, but he who clipped us kept the scissors", Sancho comes out strong and to the life:

> "For all of that," Sancho said, "when it comes to duennas there's so much to be clipped, according to what my barber tells me, that it would be better not to stir the rice even though it sticks."

Don Quixote begins as the description of a shy, timid, simple, eccentric provincial gentleman who, after the first clash with reality, develops an always growing complexity of mind that is the satisfying and diverting substance of the book. For as he goes deeper into delusion, so he is dogged by a dreadful doubt and self-knowledge. At the end, when Sancho returns home leading his master, with their roles reversed—for it is he, the realist, who has triumphed, having governed an island and having even rescued maidens in distress—Don Quixote is said to have failed in all, but to have known glory and to have won the supreme victory: victory over himself. The novel is a powerful example of the process of the growth of a work of art in a writer's mind, and of the luck of writing. For at the end of the first part which Cervantes at one time regarded as the end of the book, one can see the idea in crisis and at the point of breaking down. Some critics have thought that the irrelevant stories stuffed into the end of the First Part show a fear that the reader will be bored by the colloquies of two characters only: and that he also wished to show that he was not a mere popular writer, but could write a polished, psychological short story in the best manner of the time. (He, indeed, succeeded in the story of Don Fernando and Dorothea and, in the latter, drew a delightful analytical portrait of cleverness in women.) But in the long interval between the two parts, the idea matured and became richer in fantasy, invention and intellectual body; the range of character became wider and success—so bitterly delayed in Cervantes's life—released confident powers that delight us because they delight in themselves. Not only does Don Quixote's own case branch into its full intricacy; not only are we now taken into all the casuistries of the imaginative life; by a master stroke, Sancho is infected. The peasant gets his dream of material power, like some homely Trade Unionist, to put against the gentleman's dream of glory. Realism turns out to be as contagious to fantasy as idealism is. *Don Quixote* begins as a province, turns into Spain and ends as a universe, and far from becoming vaguer as it becomes more suggestive, it becomes earthier, more concrete, more certain in real speech and physical action. *Don Quixote* does not collapse, as the Second Part of Gogol's *Dead Souls* does, because Cervantes is not mad. He remains pragmatic, sceptical and merciful; whereas Gogol got the Russian Messianic bit between his teeth and went off his head. Spanish fantasy goes step by step with Spanish sanity. Nor, if we read *Don Quixote* truly, can it be described as a work of disillusion, if we mean by that the spiritual exhaustion which follows a great expense of spirit. The Spanish crack-up had begun, but it had only just begun. The force of that national passion was still felt. Though Cervantes was the broken soldier, though he was imprisoned, hauled before the Inquisition, and knew all the misery and confusion that the Spanish expansion abroad had left behind at home, he was not the enemy of the Spanish idea. He valued arms more than literature, as he explicitly said—incidentally in the character of Cardenio he drew an excellent portrait of a coward. What *Don Quixote* does is to enact the tragedy of experience as something still passionate though commingled with reflection: experience now more deeply felt. The comic spirit of the book is not satirical or tired, but is vital, fully engaged and positive. The wisdom runs with the events, not after them. It is stoical, not epicurean; sunlit, not eupeptic; civilised, not merely robust. *Don Quixote* bridges the gulf between two cultures, not by an inhuman cult of the people, but by excellence of intellect; by the passion a writer has for his means; by irony and love.

THE BORED BARBARIANS

IN the 'fifties Mr Anthony Powell was the first to revive the masculine traditions of English social comedy. He retrieved it on behalf of the upper classes. The joke that he is a Proust Englished by Wodehouse has something in it; in fact, the big influence was Aubrey, but where Aubrey had an almost fretful appetite for scandal and oddity, this was dignified, in Mr Powell's generation, as the belief in personal relationships. Other values, in the 'twenties and 'thirties, were in flux; one could become an anthropologist, a Malinowski of Mayfair, Bloomsbury and country-house life, and try to establish a culture pattern. I confess that I have got more out of Mr Powell's novels, as each one of them stands, than I have out of his ambition to fill out the social panorama during his period. I am not convinced that any pattern is emerging. It is enough that *A Question of Upbringing*, *The Acceptance World* and *A Buyer's Market* introduced a new kind of nerve, comic effontery and invention. They caught and played with that ineradicable core of boredom that has been the resource as well as the blight of upper-class English life, a boredom produced by the inherited genius for ironing out feelings, and doggedly covering the loss with bouts of dottiness, alcohol, adultery and class-consciousness. Mr Powell's English are punishing and punished. Their comedy has no silken threads; the threads are tweed.

What are the characteristics of this masculine tradition in our comedy? It is intelligent rather than sensitive; it is prosaic rather than poetic; it is sane rather than extravagant. It is egocentric and not a little bullying. It has manner, and that manner is ruthless and unkind. To stand up to the best manners of English society one has to be rude, exclusive and tough. One must be interested in behaviour, not in emotions; in the degree to which people hold their forts—and how much money the forts cost—not in what human beings are. The tradition begins with Fielding; it is there, minus the animal spirits, in Jane Austen. Its values are bound to the social class the writer belongs to—in Wells, for example, to the lower middle class. Hard-headed, often gifted, snobbish—for the most part—appreciative of other people's disasters and evasive about their own, self-oppressed and taking it out in horseplay and libertinage. Mr Powell's characters are a sort of club. They can listen unexhausted to gossip about each other, but their faces become suddenly masked if an outsider comes up. Their privacy is phenomenal. Widmerpool, the go-getter and man of will—a considerable comic creation—is damned because people affect not to remember whether he comes from Northamptonshire, or is it Derby? Mr Powell's narrator really hounds him. Yet, of course, Widmerpool also hounds himself.

The world Mr Powell is describing is dull, incurious and barbarous, judged from the outside, but very funny to read about. It certainly defeats foreigners. But the people of high comedy *are* generally dull. (The characters of Henry James's *Portrait of a Lady*, for example, are barely conversable.) The question is, What has Mr Powell done with them?

The early novels like *Afternoon Men* and *Venusberg* and *From a View to a Death* shared a sharp, electric, almost lyrical, performance. One of the earliest writers to expose people, and even more their way of life, by the follies of their dialogue, Mr Powell took a number of specimens of the Jazz Age and drily left little commentary. *Afternoon Men* gave one a stiff shot of party life; *Venusberg*, romantic yet lapidary, commemorated the love affair abroad; *From a View to a Death*, that social return-match: the undesirable artist among the speechless fox-hunters. Here Mr Powell's Stendhalian dryness began to warm and a deadly moralist appeared. For this is the novel of Major Fosdick, a very rare bird indeed in the English Tweedery, and one of ingenious complication. A tendency to overdress, so that even "the skin of his face was covered by small diagonal lines similar in pattern to that of his coat", was not to be attributed to any shortness of genealogy in Major Fosdick; he was far from being a stockbroker. The deep boredom and privacy of English country life had brought out something cross-gartered in his nature. He would lock himself in his dressing-room, when the fit was on, and would dress himself in a woman's evening dress and picture hat and then, taking out an exercise book, write poetry. What we so anxiously hope for indeed happens: he is caught by an enemy squire and neighbour in this rig-out and, wits not moving fast in those acres, he might have been able to palm himself off as his own wife. A moustache betrayed him.

A scene of this kind is, of course, a stock one in farce and it is funny enough as it stands. But everything lies in the handling and here we see the first signs of Mr Powell's coming maturity. He is never satisfied with a mere joke. The encounter has two beauties: first that Fosdick compromises. He takes off the picture hat and swings it absurdly as he talks; second, neither man mentions his astonishment or horror, but treats the whole episode *à l'anglaise*, as a test of character and upbringing. Fosdick knows he will have now to surrender in the long row over his pheasants. He retires, stiff in the upper lip, to a nursing home in the proper way. Mr Passenger, the squire, will go home and, as is proper, forbid his daughters the house, but he too recognises moral defeat. He had considered himself a man of independent genius whose luck was always out, a potential superman who had never had his chance. His tragedy is that:

> In this moment of emergency he had been thrown back on the old props of tradition and education and when he might have enjoyed a substantial revenge he had behaved with all the restraint in the world.

The characters in *From a View to a Death* are perennial in the classical English comedy of country life and the national mixture is there, even to the mad cynicism of the cautionary tale. I am thinking of the barrel organ players who appealed for charity on the grounds that they were orphans.

> The postulation rested wholly on the handicap of loss of parents, which because the youngest of the orphans must have been at least forty years of age, was in their case presumed to have persisted into early middle life.

But if the characters are the same, the observation is revised. They are done in new colours. Mr Powell is, as I have said, devoted to Aubrey's *Lives* and his comedy has behind it a stolid native melancholy that is terrifyingly full-blooded. He has wit, but it is not rapier-play; rather it leaves a skilful boxer's marks upon the body of the enemy. The characters retire bruised, not nicked, from the ring. And then an unusual dimension is added to his people: they are reconsidered. They are not only figures of fun and amusement; they have a serious relation to their own experience or to the author's, so that we are shown the comedy of social history.

In a world in which standards and values have vanished, to what do we turn? To the attempt to find out a personal pattern—that favourite word of unbelieving anthropologists—to the sober technical question as to where we were accurate and where (through immaturity) off the mark in the consideration of ourselves, our friends and our world. We become the pedants of the cult of personal relationships.

This pedantry is the basis of Mr Powell's new comedies. *A Buyer's Market* reconsiders the characters of *A Question of*

Upbringing and both books fill in at length the social scene that was left out in *Afternoon Men*. So we have a finely painted, detailed picture of the last year at Eton, the London Season, the first ventures in society, the first stages of a career; and in the background the upper classes start on that peculiar course of chasing after artists, drifting into Bohemia, the demi-monde and the business rackets, which has been typical of our age. *A Buyer's Market* contains three absurd figures from this time: Mr Deacon the ageing bad painter, Uncle Giles the shady rebel, and the superb Widmerpool whom we had first seen at Eton—wronged, earnest, narrowed and ambitious. Widmerpool is a wonderful portrait of the go-getting young man—he is Fielding's Blifil, but now in business—whose pursuit of the main chance has given a growing squint to his life. He talks like a Pep book, he calculates absurdly aloud, he is prone to social disasters of the first magnitude. He is not debagged by the young oafs at the debs' ball, but he does get covered with castor sugar; it is he who is made to pay for the Free Love girl's abortion; it is he who drives his car into the ornamental urn at the magnate's castle and who makes a ludicrous appearance behind the bars in the dungeon there. Widmerpool never comes up smiling; muttered indignation attends his injuries. He becomes the victim one cannot love, crouching round the ashes of his private shames, but he has his own private laugh. For his pursuit of private respectability and the windy justifications of the yes-man is always successful.

The farce of Widmerpool gains from the sententious, slow motion manner of Mr Powell's writing. The deb sprinkles Widmerpool lightly with the sugar pot:

> More from surprise than because she wished additionally to torment him, Barbara did not remove her hand before the whole contents of the vessel—which voided itself in an instant of time—had descended upon his head and

> shoulders, covering him with sugar more completely than might have been thought possible in so brief a space. Widmerpool's rather sparse hair had been liberally greased with a dressing—the sweetish smell of which I remembered as somewhat disagreeable when applied in France—this lubricant retaining the grains of sugar, which, as they adhered thickly to his skull, gave him the appearance of having turned white with shock at a single stroke, which judging by what could be seen of his expression, he might very well in reality have done underneath the glittering incrustations that enveloped his head and shoulders. He had writhed sideways to avoid the downpour, and a cataract of sugar had entered the space between neck and collar; yet another jet streaming between eyes and spectacles.

Mr Powell is excellent with the raffish. Some critics have objected to his sententious manner; but even if it is true that this is what happens to Proust if one drains off sensibility and makes him appropriate to clubs, I think the sententious irony succeeds. It is, after all, native and part of the tradition. It adds a very English flavour either of comic tautology or deflation.

> "Shall we leave the gentlemen to their port?" said Mrs Widmerpool, when finally the subject had been picked bone dry.
>
> She mouthed the words "gentlemen" and "port" as if they might be facetiously disputable as strictly literal descriptions in either case.

That final "in either case" is the devastating torpedo. Mr Powell may have got overfond of phrases like "in his case" and all those "unquestionablys", "alternativelys", "undoubtedlys" and "if anythings", but in their forensic malice, they rub the salt in hard. (The narrator's desire to pass as the impartial norm conceals a fierce melancholy which I suppose to be Mr Powell's energising wound as an artist.) The habit of labouring a point may also at last add the macabre to the grotesque:

> A direct hit had excised even the ground floor, so that the basement was revealed as a sunken garden, or site of archaeological excavations long abandoned, where great sprays of willowherb and ragwort flowered through the paving stones; only a few broken milk bottles and a laceless boot recalling contemporary life.

And the deliberate intellectualisation of an absurdity may become disturbing:

> The name Casanova's Chinese Restaurant offered one of those unequivocal blendings of disparate elements of the imagination which suggest a whole new state of mind or way of life.

These words come from *Casanova's Chinese Restaurant.* The story has two musicians, three writers, a painter, a biography-writing peeress, a left-wing peer turning intellectual; we may find ourselves in a country house like Dogdene, a discarded first or second wife may drag us down to Earls Court or Pimlico.

The aim of Mr Powell's sententiousness is to appal by the judicious: in a sense, his comedy is hysterical. There are several references, in this novel, to a ghost train the narrator and his friends used to go on when they were young; and it is implied that their lives, in the Bohemian period he is describing, have been like this absurd and finally ghastly journey.

But these novels constitute a *roman fleuve.* The same characters reappear, with new wives, husbands, careers, fortunes and fates; they are connected intimately in their social set. They live in a whispering gallery, in a mocking music of echoes from the past. They astonish one another by their unpredictable actions and their new chummings-up. Who would have thought, in *At Lady Molly's*, that Widmerpool would fall for that brassy ex-VAD, Mrs Haycock? Or, in *Casanova's Chinese Restaurant*, that the grand Mrs Fox would take up with a ballet dancer and shower him with presents? Here a difficulty arises. After the deep state of their early flow, such novels run into shallows. What began as a panorama begins to sound like a gossip column. One noticed this in *At Lady Molly's*; in *Casanova's Chinese Restaurant*, the habit of gossip has really set in and the central interest—the examination of two marriages—is not strong enough to stop it. One has the irritating impression that Jenkins, the narrator, has no other profession but to run about collecting the news; his stability has become fitful. The characters exchange too much hearsay. This is the danger with the *roman fleuve* when it lacks a strongly sustaining idea beyond the convenience of its own existence. I am not sure that the idea of the decadence of a class anecdotally viewed is strong enough. I think Mr Powell has now to guard against the risk that his characters will be so familiar and real to him that he will cease to make them important to us; that they will lose their true strength, *i.e.* that they are obsessive fictions. The constant difficulty of the novelist is to avoid the engaging demimonde that lies between art and life. Hearsay enfeebles, if Aubrey's brief emblematic lives become Aubrey's long ones.

Against this natural drift Mr Powell puts his set comic scenes and uses, of course, his notable organising powers. But, in *Casanova's Chinese Restaurant*, there is only one of these comic set pieces strong enough to stand against the current. It must be said that this particular one is as good as any he has done; it is the scene in which the drunken Stringham mocks the nagging out of the tragic Maclintick's terrible wife, and is himself finally carried off by his old governess. It is marvellously observed and the tragic sequel is all the more forceful for it; one notices here how brilliantly Mr Powell arranges material that has become immense. He is very accomplished in pulling things up out of the past and planting them massively before us. I put this scene beside the earlier one in *At Lady Molly's* where the General, newly come to psychological studies, makes his absurd, slow-motion diagnosis of Widmerpool's sexual misfortune. Mr Powell is a master of such refracted comedy and that is where the sheer intelligence of the masculine school counts. Such things are far superior to his social commentary.

In praising Mr Powell for his hard-headed comedy, his mastery of burlesque and farce, I do not undervalue his serious reflections. He is not diffused by urbanity. He is misanthropic, sane, experienced; there is no cynicism. His epigrams are withering but they do not utterly demolish. Their balance is as formidable as their wit:

> He also lacked that subjective, ruthless love of presiding over other people's affairs which often makes basically heartless people adept at offering effective consolation.

He has a sense of proportion, yet he also has edge. It is an uncommon pair of gifts. When one speaks of his melancholy one is not describing a passive condition; one is speaking of a driving force. His almost geological utterances suggest that even Mayfair and Pimlico have their Egdon Heaths:

> Love had received one of those shattering jolts to which it is peculiarly vulnerable from extraneous circumstances.

A sentence like that could go on the title-page of *Casanova's Chinese Restaurant*. It contains, down to the very word "peculiarly", the undertones and overtones of this novelist, in whose work the human comedy is grimly engrained.

MEREDITH'S BRAINSTUFF

DOES anyone know what to think of Meredith's novels now? I think not. The lack of sympathy is complete. Difficult to read in his own time, he is almost impenetrable to ourselves. "Full of good brainstuff", Gissing said of *Diana of the Crossways*, and added joyfully that the true flavour of this book came out only after three readings! It was Meredith's brain that annoyed his early critics; today we suspect his heart. Insincerity and freakishness are held against him. Yet, we ought to feel some contact, for he is the first modern highbrow novelist in the sense of being the first to write for the minority and to be affected, even if unconsciously, by the split in our culture. George Eliot, his rival intellectual, was not so affected.

Those who visited the chalet at Box Hill in the period of Meredith's old age and fame were astonished by the mass of French novels there. He set out, as the French do, to facet life so that it became as hard as a diamond, to shape it by Idea. (At the time of the death of his second wife, he wrote: "I see all round me how much Idea governs", and Idea was "the parent of life as opposed to that of perishable blood".) The notion sometimes gave an intellectual dignity to his creations, but just as often dignity was merely stance. For Meredith's imagination housed the most ill-assorted ideas: there was dandyism, there was the oracular Romance of his claim to be a Celt, there was the taste for German fantasy, the feeling for supermen and women and the heroic role of the fittest. If we follow his own habit of metaphorical association, we find ourselves saying that the descendant of two generations of naval and military tailors in Portsmouth was born to the art of dressing-up. In fact, his grandfather, and his father before him, had been as fantastic in their lives as he was in his novels; the son was able to survive his own self-deceptions by the aid of wit. The difficulty of Meredith does not lie in his thought, but in its conceits, in the flowered waistcoats of his intellectual wardrobe. Gosse used to object to this passage from the description of a scene at the gaming table:

> He compared the creatures dabbling over the board to summer flies on butcher's meat, periodically scared by a cloth. More in the abstract, they were snatching at a snap-dragon bowl. It struck him that the gamblers had thronged on an invitation to drink the round of seed-time and harvest in a gulp. Again they were desperate gleaners, hopping, skipping, bleeding, amid a whizz of scythe blades, for small wisps of booty. Nor was it long before the presidency of an ancient hoary Goat-Satan might be perceived with skew-eyes and pucker-mouth, nursing a hoof on a tree. Our medieval Enemy sat symbolical in his deformities, as in old Italian and Dutch thick-line engravings of him. He rolled a ball for souls, excited like kittens, to catch it tumbling into the dozens of vacant pits.

Brainstuff, indeed. For our welfare (Meredith warned us) Life was always trying to pull us away from consciousness and brainstuff. On the other hand, "Matter that is not nourishing to brains can help to constitute nothing but the bodies that are pitched on rubbish heaps." Human felicity is always trying (he said in a letter) to kill consciousness. There is often an extraordinary violence in Meredith's neo-pagan metaphors.

Meredith, like Browning, had too many ideas. And, as in his novels, so in his life, the brilliant egoist appeared to be an artificial construction. An American biographer, Professor Lionel Stevenson, notes in *The Ordeal of George Meredith* that by the time he was fifty, Meredith "had completely molded himself in a dramatic personality". He had become the Comic Spirit in person and if there was overstrain, it was for clear personal reasons: "The components had been collected with a kind of genius. Impenetrably screened behind it lurked the Portsmouth tailor shop, the bankrupt father, and the dreadful decade of his first marriage." The price was that he did not inspire intimacy:

> It was not that he seemed either aloof or insincere; but he created the effect of a perpetual and consummate theatrical performance and the pilgrims to Box Hill were not so much consorting with a friend as they were appreciating a unique work of art.

It would be misleading to continue to press a comparison between Meredith's life and his work as a novelist. Professor Stevenson is concerned with the writing life and very little with literary criticism. He comments on the novels, as they come along, but does not examine them in much detail. He notes (what Henry James deplored) Meredith's evasion of the *scène à faire*; for example, it is the point of all Meredith's novels, as Professor Stevenson admirably says, that the chief characters shall be tried by ordeal. They are burned in the fire of their own tragic or comic illusions and emerge from self-deception into self-knowledge. Yet, in *Diana of the Crossways*, the scene where Diana commits the folly of letting a political secret out of the bag is skipped. Is she an hysterical egoist? Is she as immoral as she appears? Has she merely lost her head? Only a direct account of the scene at the newspaper office, where she hands over the secret, can tell us. Meredith was no story-teller—a fatal defect, above all in the days of the three-volume novel. He is a novelist who gesticulates about a story that is implicitly already told. The cage of character is his interest. The rest of Professor Stevenson's criticism is appreciative but not considerable. I find only one point of disagreement. He says that Meredith was the first to introduce something close to natural dialogue in the English novel. Certainly Meredith breaks the convention in which dialogue had been written up to his time; the result is not natural speech. Meredith simply applied his own allusiveness to dialogue, and allusiveness happens to be a characteristic of ordinary speech anyway; he was too full of himself to see the characters or speech of other people, except in so far as they could be elaborated as "idea" and in stylised form. Meredith's dialogue is simply Meredith cutting a figure in his own society.

As a biography Professor Stevenson's *Life* tells a well-known story competently. A writer has not much time for living and Meredith's life is one more variant on the theme of the calamities of authorship. There is the aloof, handsome, snobbish youth making that first break with his environment by sheer pride of obsession. There is the unhappy marriage to Peacock's daughter and the hardening of the heart—yet Meredith's heart must have hardened in childhood. And then the literary grind follows. *The Ordeal of Richard Feverel* is a failure, so is *Evan Harrington. Harry Richmond* gets a few admirers. His integrity was untouched by neglect; he worked without a public until he was fifty, and by that time, his health went to pieces. The tall, eagle-faced man, the non-stop wit, talker and laugher, with his bouts of "manly" boisterousness and back-slapping, had always been a dyspeptic. Now he suddenly became deaf. He presently had the symptoms of locomotor ataxia. To keep his family he had ground away for years as a publisher's reader and wrote three articles a week for a provincial newspaper. For years also he made a small annual sum by reading to an old lady once a week. His letters are full of the groans of laborious authorship. At fifty he had had enough, but he was fated to live into his eighties, unable to hear speech or music; unable to walk, which had been his chief pleasure in life. He was drawn about in a donkey chair. He was sixty before he became famous; the relative comfort of his old age was only in part due to his success—he inherited a little money from an aunt. In his personal life, he had seen the death of his two wives and the son whom he had once adored, but who had become estranged from him after his second marriage. A psychologist might say that Meredith's life is an ironical illustration of the theory that we get what we are conditioned to desire. The death of his mother in very early childhood, and the pride and fecklessness of his father, had formed Meredith for self-sufficiency and loneliness: the brain rapidly filled in the hollows left by affections which had been denied. His own affections certainly became intellectual; his love letters are clearly of the kind that exhaust the feeling in an excessive flow of lyrical expression. He grieved over the death of his wife, but he *had* compared her to a mud fort! Friends found an annoying disconnection between brain and heart. There was one reward. It seems frequently to come to the egoistic temperament: the exciting, if heartless, power of living in the present. He tore up old letters and, in old age, is said to have scorned the common consolation of that time: living in the past. The torrential talker, the magician, was in short a picturesque monster, relishing his scars. One whimsical young American admirer —mentioned by Professor Stevenson—made the shrewd, even Meredithean remark, that he would probably have been happier and better organised if he had been a woman.

To return to the unreadableness of Meredith. He is not unreadable; he exists a page at a time; he is quotable, to be skipped through. The large characters like Sir Willoughby Patterne or Richmond Roy, are myths. Meredith is tedious only in his detail; when he intends to be preposterous he is wonderful, as he is in that scene in *Harry Richmond*, where Richmond Roy poses publicly as an equestrian statue.

Meredithean irony is excessive, as all the brainstuff is, but it is excellent when the character or the scene is fantastic enough for him. He is impossible until one submits to his conception of Romance; after that he is only hard work. He is a rhapsodist who writes about people who are really souls moving impatiently out of their present into their future, towards destruction or self-knowledge. They are pagan souls in the poetic sense, not characters in the moralistic sense; giants of the Celtic tradition, grotesques in the German; all their geese are swans. Their lives are portrayed as heightened exercises in their integrity and their sense of honour. Professor Stevenson remarks that Meredith was attacked with ridicule until he was fifty, not only because he was a pagan who could not tell a story and at odds with popular realism, but because Romance was out. His fame began when Romance came in. Stevenson and Conrad contain strange echoes. Chesterton's suburban romance owes a lot to him. D. H. Lawrence was the last to be influenced by him. Another element in making his fame was the rise of feminism. It is very hard for ourselves to imagine another revival in Romance. What a future generation of novelists may find stimulating in him is that preoccupation of his with that he called "the idea". He enlarged the novel with a brilliant power of generalisation. It was spoiled, as so much English fiction has been, by the obsession with romantic class-consciousness, but in *Beauchamp's Career*, or even in a clumsy novel like *One of Our Conquerors*, he has an ability to generalise about society as living history. And his presentation of character—Diana Merion, for example, in *Diana of the Crossways*—as idea and person at once, is a fertile addition to the old English tradition of character types, removed from our moralising habit. The pile of French novels at the chalet, the attempt to turn Molière into English, had their point.

Harry Richmond contains fewer difficulties of style than

most of his work, chiefly because it is written in the first person. Meredith was a poetic or rhapsodic novelist, and *Harry Richmond* is a romance about the serious deceits and comedies of romance. Several of the characters are more than life-size, or speak and live in the heightened language of an imagination which is sometimes fine, at other times wooden or uncertain of its level; but there is no doubt that Meredith creates a complete world. Critics have often said that Meredith's taste for the chivalrous and high-sounding takes him clean out of the nineteenth century and sends his novels floating away in clouds of non-existent history. They have said that we can never pin him down to time and place, and that he is intellectually Ruritanian. This is only superficially true. We must take into consideration a novelist's temperament before we judge like that. Because Meredith's mind was microscopic, because his subject again and again is people's imaginative, ideal, future-consuming view of themselves and of their environment, this does not mean that they have no known place in a recognisable world. Nothing could be more thoroughly Victorian in imagination that *Harry Richmond*; if the neo-medieval colouring is precisely that, this novel reads as if it were an attempt to glamorise Victorian life out of recognition. This is a well-known habit among the poets of the nineteenth century. The cult of the picturesque history can be described as an escape from the grim squalor of the industrial revolution; but we can also think of it as a confident and imperial enterprise of colonisation. The Victorians were high-feeders on what is felt to be foreign in time or place. *Harry Richmond* is cast in the imperial frame of mind, and if Meredith can be justly accused of being merely Ruritanian, he did not fall into the ludicrous which so often imperils (shall we say?) Tennyson's historical or legendary poems. The very pretences of Harry Richmond's fantastic father to the throne of England and to royal blood expresses the rising, exuberant side of the situation in England at that time when people were very liable to be plethoric about the greatness of their history. The plot and many details of narration are also true to the period. It was a time of violent changes of fortune in private life, of tremendous claims to estates and titles. Meredith is known to have got the idea for Richmond Roy's wild claim from the fact that William the Fourth had many children by an Irish actress, and also from the marriage of George IV to Mrs Fitzherbert. Meredith's remoteness has been greatly exaggerated by critics brought up on realism.

The spell of *Harry Richmond*—for to read it is to pass into trance—exists because of the brilliant handling of an impossible subject. If Meredith had confronted Richmond Roy's claim squarely and realistically he would have been lost. His art lies in building up the character of the father as the romantic and charming figure seen by his child, and then in gradually disclosing that he is first an adventurer, living in state one minute and in a debtor's prison the next; at last, by evasive insinuation, comes the royal claim. Richmond Roy grows larger and larger, richer in resource and effrontery, more and more triumphant for every setback, but skating on thinner and thinner ice the farther he goes. Meredith learned from French novelists the method of working up to the key phrase. The moment the farmers on whom Harry Richmond is boarded when he is a child start deferring to him, and are heard at last to whisper superstitiously "Blood rile" the thrill is aesthetic. It has exactly the effect of the words "You are an egoist" when they are spoken to Sir Willoughby Patterne and when they transform the tension and tighten the focus of that book. Richmond Roy has been too obviously compared with Micawber; he is far more complex than that; his follies and dreams have genius. He is not a windbag; he is a fine actor. He is nearer to Falstaff. Richmond Roy alarms.

He alarms when he brazenly orders scarlet liveries, permitted only to the Royal Family, for his postilions. He alarms by his knowledge of our weaknesses. He can bounce his way into buying a chateau or a yacht. He can spellbind a foreign court and rout the hostess of Bath. Notoriety he thrives on. His impudence when he poses as an equestrian statue at the German court is splendid. These imaginative episodes set off the scurvy ones; the father's nasty relationships with the press, his unscrupulous robbery of his adoring son, his caddish exploitation of the young man's love for the German princess, his cold-hearted swindling of his sister-in-law. He pretends that the money came from personages who are anxious to keep him quiet. He is a mountebank, and if we are glad in the end that Squire Beltham exposes him in good Squire Western style, it is not really because we like to see vice punished, but because the rogue has got too maddening and has reached an hysterical and pathetic stage where he will become a figure too farcical to bear his real weight as a symbol; hence his tragedy. Meredith works up to that proper conclusion but, like a great artist, explores all the other possibilities first. He has the piling-on instinct of the story-teller. We are delighted towards the end when Richmond Roy is confronted with another false claimant, a so-called Dauphin who claims to have marks on his body which prove his heredity. Meredith is clever enough to give this episode twice; in two different kinds of gossip, one showing Richmond Roy the master of an insulting situation, the other through Squire Beltham's hilarious British scorn. Meredith's mastery of comedy does not exclude the low and, indeed, in the low he is not tempted to his vice of over-polishing. When the ladies retire from the dinner table—a nice touch that—the squire lets go:

> They got the two together, William. Who are you? I'm a Dauphin; who are you? I'm Ik Dine, bar sinister. Oh,

says the other; then I take precedence of you! Devil a bit, says the other; I've got more spots than you. Proof, says one. You first, t'other. Count, one cries. T'other sings out. Measles. Better than a dying Dauphin, roars t'other; and swore both of 'em 'twas nothing but port wine stains and pimples. Ha! Ha! And, William, will you believe it?—the couple went round begging the company to count spots to prove their big birth. Oh Lord, I'd ha' paid a penny to be there! A Jack of Bedlam Ik Dine damned idiot!—makes the name o' Richmond stink.

It has been said that Meredith is not a story-teller—but a story need not depend very much on plot; it can and does in Meredith depend on pattern and the disclosure of character through events. The weakness is that the fantastic father ngrosses the great part of the interesting incident; when he is off-stage our interest flags. Meredith's narrative is not a straight line; it is a meandering back and forth in time, a blending of events and commentary and this Meredith must have gone for instinctively, because he is wooden in straightforward narration. We follow an imagination that cannot bear precision. He depends on funking scenes, on an increasing uncertainty about how exactly events did occur. There is a refusal to credit reality with importance until it has been parcelled out between two or three minds and his own reflections on it. Even in the duel scene in Germany, the excellence is due to the ironical telescoping of the event; we are hearing Meredith on the duel, telling us what to look at and what not to bother about. The effect is of jumping from one standstill scene to another. Life is not life, for him, until it is over; until it is history. (One sees this method in the novels of William Faulkner.) The movement is not from event to event, but from situation to situation, and in each situation there is a kernel of surprising incident. In realism he is tedious. One can almost hear him labouring at what he does not believe in and depending on purely descriptive skill.

The love scenes in *Harry Richmond* present a double difficulty to ourselves. The mixture of realism and high romance is awkward; we are made to feel the sensuality of lovers in a way remarkable to mid-Victorian novels; their words appear to be a highfalutin' way of taking the reader's mind off it and, in this respect, Meredith's pagan idealism is no more satisfactory than the conventional Christian idealism of other novelists. Like Scott, Meredith is always better at the minor lovers than the major ones. His common sense, touched by a half-sympathetic scorn, is truer than his desire, which is too radiantly egocentric. In Meredith's personal life, his strongest and spontaneous feelings of love were those of a son and a father, and this is, of course, the theme of *Harry Richmond.* That is why, more than any of his other works, this one appears to be rooted in a truth about the human heart. In erotic love, Meredith never outgrew his early youth and the fact over-exhilarates and vulgarises him by turns.

Harry Richmond is thought to be less encumbered than Meredith's other novels because it is written in the first person. Unfortunately, as Mr Percy Lubbock pointed out some years ago in *The Craft of Fiction*, the first person has to be both narrator and actor in his own story, and in consequence stands in his own light. I do not believe that this is a serious fault in *Harry Richmond* as a story, for what carries us forward is Meredith's remarkable feeling for the generosity, impulsiveness and courage of youth and its splendid blindness to the meaning of its troubles. Harry is blinded by romantic love for his father and the German princess; he is weak in not facing the defects of the former and in not being "great" enough for the latter; but both these sets of behaviour are honourable and have our sympathy. With his father he shares a propensity for illusion and romance and is cured of them. Since he is the narrator we have only his word for it, and one is far from convinced that Harry Richmond has been cured or even examined. Put the story in Henry James's hands and one sees at once that the whole question of illusion or romance would have been gone into far more deeply. It is the old Meredithean trouble; he is an egoistical writer, fitted out with the egoistical accomplishments, and one who can never be sufficiently unselfed to go far into the natures of others. His portraits start from him, not from them, and the result is that he is only picturesque, a master of ear and eye, a witty judge of the world, a man a good deal cutting a figure in his own society; we are given brilliant views of the human heart, but we do not penetrate it. He has no sense of the calamitous, no sense of the broken or naked soul, and—fatally—no sense of evil. More than any other novelist of his age, he has the Victorian confidence and in a manner so dazzling and profuse that it is natural they called him Shakespearean. In the effusive Victorian sense, he was; but Shakespearean merely linguistically, glamorously, at second hand, without any notion of human life as passion or of suffering as more than disappointment. He is a very literary novelist indeed.

CONRAD

CONRAD exists in English literature, but he is a harsh exotic who can never quite be assimilated to our modes. No English novelist has his peculiar accent in psychological and moral curiosity; it is like the knowing accent of Kipling, a foreigner's acquired slang, but expressing a far more elevated sensibility than Kipling had; only Henry James, another alien, with his pursuit of fine consciousness, approaches Conrad's fencing with extremes. Yet here all Conrad's critics have been dissatisfied. They have felt, as Forster did, that he was following extremes into a fog of argument or rhetoric; or they have been obliged to agree with the comment of Dr Leavis—the most substantial of Conrad's critics—on the inequalities of *Heart of Darkness* and that

> he is intent on making a virtue out of not knowing what he means. The vague and unrealisable, he asserts with a strained impressiveness, is the profoundly and tremendously significant.

Even in *Nostromo*, where Conrad's powers of concretion were married to a great subject, we shall not exactly know where we stand. We are always liable in his work to lapse from the certainties of art into the restless brilliance of opinion, to find the matter in hand being explored with the cleverness of the café writer and the moral dilettante. We shall be haunted by the special and tragic brilliance of the exile who, as he exhibts himself and plays his role, is never unconscious of the fact. As Mr Douglas Hewitt says in *Conrad: A Reassessment*, his novels are not tragedies—they *resemble* tragedies. They are, generally speaking, one must add, inhibited from tragic fullness by his famous, defensive and histrionic irony. He is, at bottom, a rather sadistic and sardonic writer. His irony is ultimately perverse—or, as earlier critics used to say, morbid—because it is a personal irony and does not always lie in the nature of the events he describes. Is *Nostromo* a great classical novel or a brilliant commentary? That is to say, superb as it is, does it not strike one as being a commentary on the kind of novel or dramatic work that could, at some time, be written on its subject?

Nostromo is the most strikingly modern of Conrad's novels. It might have been written in 1954 and not, as it was, in 1904. All the issues of the economic exploitation of a backward country are here; the politics of Costa-guana over two or three generations are telescoped in depth without losing the focus on the present. We see both the ideal and fraud in colonial exploitation, in the fight for liberalism, progress, reform, the bent to revolution and the advent of a foreign power. Even the rise of two of the now dominant forces in his kind of situation is clearly noted: the desire of America to take over everything in the world and, against or with that, the rise of the masses. Conrad did not set these things down in a political or historical essay, nor in a novel of propaganda, but in the impure detail of a large sceptical and imaginative work. Every moment is physically realised not by a right-minded and insensitive political reporter with a mind hardened-off (or softened) by his programme, but by an artist dealing, as art must, in the waste, the elusive, the incalculable. It is one of the prophetic felicities of this work that it is pervaded by a profound, even morbid sense of insecurity which is the very spirit of our age, and that sense is (as it must always be) personal. Before anyone else—though we may pause to give Mr E. M. Forster his due—Conrad the exile foresaw that in half a century we should all become exiles, in a sense.

One or two reflections follow from our astonishment with *Nostromo*. The first is a general reflection on the social soil in which the modern English novel is planted. The great English subject—one is inclined to say—and at any rate the great subject which includes a picture of society, lies outside England, simply because English life itself has for long been parasitic on life abroad and does not wish to recognise the fact. "Abroad" is where English institutions have been put to the test and not in South Wales, Tyneside, Birmingham or Surrey. As I say, apart from Conrad, only E. M. Forster seems to have known this; possibly Lawrence, too, in a book like *Kangaroo*. The second reflection is one that throws a light on some of Conrad's defects as a novelist. He suffers from being before his proper time. It is a freak of time that he is a Romantic. Even in small yet not unimportant matters like the use of dialogue, Conrad was unlucky. If he could be writing *The Secret Agent* or the bandit pages of *Victory* now, he would certainly not write the wooden Cockney or the ludicrous melodrama of his gangster's dialogue; the intellectual energies of the refugee would not have been spent on acquiring literary English, but the English of speech.

Conrad is a man in what we may call the post-1940 situation, but who is obliged to conceal the fact under a dramatic fog of rhetoric. He loved rhetoric, of course, and became—as Mr Hewitt says—more prone to it when his talent went to pieces from *Chance* onwards; vaguely emotive words like "unspeakable", "nameless", "inscrutable", "horror", "pure evil", "mystery", "Woman" are the well-known pedals of the Romantic organ. Behind them lay things which, a generation or so after, he could have named, and as an incipient nihilist he would have been bound to name them. He would have been obliged to live or set down in precise physical detail, the nihilism which he feared so much in his nature. It would have been drawn out by a nihilist age. The case of Kurz in *Heart of Darkness*, the case of Heyst in *Victory*, or Decoud in *Nostromo*, is contemporary, but now the full glare of the interrogator's lamp is on their faces. Conrad would have been drawn out of the grandiloquent shadows that exasperate us and which seem to exasperate him; he would have found less to opine upon and more, cruelly, to state. The morbidity of which early critics complained—quite rightly; before 1914 certain values seemed impregnable—would not strike one in our imaginary Conrad who had been drawn out by times that would fit his temperament like a glove. Betrayal, guilt, isolation, the double self, corruption, the undisguised sadism that has appeared in our life, the anarchy, are not matters of speculation and pious lament. They are contemporary facts.

Mr Hewitt is of the opinion that the decline of Conrad's work which began with *Chance*, comes from a failure to see any secure or positive values which could counter the force of his negative criticism. The alternative was to plump for popular Romance and an unreal, black and white world of wholly good or wholly evil people. These later books are simply the early rhetoric expanded. Mr Hewitt's book is a short one which sticks to the text of a few of the novels and is concerned with the specific moral health of Conrad's genius at different times; it is far from comprehensive and though its main points are excellent, one misses a sensibility to detail. Gould and his wife, for example, are hardly realised characters in *Nostromo*: they are states of mind, like the Dukes who hold the Court in a Shakespearean drama. Why in comparison does Mr Hewitt find Heyst's conversations with the girl on the island less acceptable than Mrs Gould's conversations with Decoud in *Nostromo*? The dialogue is wooden in both instances but the matter is allusive and subtle. Is not the difference between Gould and Heyst simply that one is a practical and obsessed solitary scheming for his mine, whereas Heyst is a passive solitary? Mr Hewitt warns us of the danger of paraphrasing Conrad, but Conrad paraphrases himself in characters like Gould, Heyst and Decoud. They are attitudes, not people, though they are attitudes lit up here and there by the novelist's power to give them flashes of individual life. The fact is that Conrad was a writer of restless and changeable conceptions, but he was poor in invention. His imaginative eye did not easily move; it was fixed upon brilliant detail so that the sound of a thing like the clank of railway trucks, with its suggestion of prisoner's fetters, becomes so powerful as an image, that it is more real to us than the people who have to be explained or "talked on" in brilliant but ultimately elusive colloquies. He is a jumpy, attitudinising, artificial writer, bedevilled by his eye. The selection of the isolated subject is, in part, the expression of his maddened desire for a subject that can be made to stand still so that it can be forcibly elaborated. The pattern of *Nostromo* is wonderful. It is like some grim brocade; yet was it necessary to be so elaborate in order to get the utmost out of the subject? And did Conrad get the utmost? On the level of a great tragic conception, I think, it must at last be thought he did not. We are overburdened by detail, by a too constant intensity. We are hypnotised. We "come to", but there has been no purgation.

The Secret Sharer, in Mr Hewitt's opinion, marks the deciding crisis in Conrad's life as a novelist. In this excellent tale he thinks Conrad exorcised his personal devil and thereafter turned away from the central conflict which had fertilised his art. Leggatt, the man who takes refuge in the young Captain's cabin, has killed a man in some squabble, and he plays the part of the Dostoevskian "double" as Gentleman Brown had done to Lord Jim. Leggatt is the hidden transgressor in the unconscious, an embodiment of the fear "that there are parts of himself which he has not yet brought into the light of day" and which may interfere "with the ideal conception of one's own personality every man sets up for himself secretly". The Captain is put to a strain leading almost to madness by his secret partnership and actually risks his ship; but having pushed the pact to the limit, he conquers and sails off, free at last, where Kurtz, Gentleman Brown of *Nostromo* and Lord Jim represent failures in this struggle with the unconscious. It is a shrewd point of Mr Hewitt's that *Chance*, with its optimism of black-and-white Romance and reliance on the sailor's simple code immediately follows these histories of failure. Conrad's pessimism, his lack of a positive scheme of spiritual values, clearly left him, as a Romantic artist, in an intolerable situation.

Exile, the fact of being uncommitted, is at the bottom of Conrad's triumphs and his failures. He is a writer of great vanity. One has the impression of a writer more suited to the theatre than to the novel. The wonderful faceting of *Nostromo* is essentially theatrical in effect; self-consciousness, artifice, the sense of his role which every Conrad character feels, including Marlow himself, strengthen our impression. Of course, he was no more a dramatist than Henry James was, but there is this straining towards the drama. It is, indeed, the self-dramatising, evasive, speculative quality in his own comments on his work which make him an unusually unreliable guide to his achievement.

Two things strike us about Conrad. The first is that despite his life of action, his true heritage was political and literary. He took to the sea, as a writer might, if he had a good stomach, out of a romantic passion for travel and geography. He was not a born seaman who eventually takes to writing as another form of extroversion. Conrad's father was a well-known if minor literary figure in Poland, a dilettante of reckless political nerve, and the son's decision to go to sea was a violent break with the formative influences of his upbringing. It was a protest, an adventure, could almost be thought an aberration, and was likely to recoil. Secondly, we must note the immense importance of politics and especially of political defeat in his life. He saw defeat lived out in tragedy, in the death of his father and mother after their exile in Russia. He was with them there; he nearly died there. He learned exile as a child. The "gloom" of Conrad was not the broad, passive gloom of the Russians which seems to arise from the dull excess of space; he disliked being called a Slav. He was a Westerner who despised the Dostoevskian Russian. Conrad's "gloom"—as his biographer says—began with his early schooling in sorrow. It grew, later on, into something hard and sardonic. It is the bitter irony of the active man of strong imagination who sees, with personal indignation, the relativeness of experience. The exile has the illusion of moral freedom and becomes a connoisseur of the ironies of his situation.

There is some parallel in the lives of Conrad and his father. The dangerous political gestures of the father were patriotic, noble, passionate and romantic, but they were carried on in the futile void created by an all-powerful tyranny. There was a total lack of prospect. It was oceanic. In the life of the son the conception of tyranny that wastes life has changed into the embittering notion of Destiny. There is something odd about Conrad's idea of Destiny; so often it is merely exasperating, when it should surely be dreadful; perverse when it should be impassive. The men of the generation of Conrad's father knew evil by direct experience. The police rapped on the door. The arrest was made. The lies were told. The trial took place and the protests. The sentence to Siberia, which was really a sentence to fatal illness and the loss of everything valued in life, was a fact—to Conrad's father. To the son, when he grew up, evil was a bad dream, a sinister memory, a dark rhetorical suggestion. Again and again in his work, the evil thing becomes diffused and generalised into an indefinable reek of corruption. Indeed Conrad's special contribution to the English novel, is to have insinuated into it the sense of an atmosphere of evil which is notoriously lacking; but as Dr Leavis has fairly said: "he is intent on making a virtue out of not knowing what he means. The vague and unrealisable, he asserts with a strained impressiveness, is the profoundly and tremendously significant." On the other hand, we have to note that Conrad is better at the evil fact—the cannibal helmsman lying dead in the wheelhouse in *Heart of Darkness*; the crew disappointed that they cannot eat the body—than he is at evil in the general sense. There are times when the belief in original sin sounds either histrionic or professional; and in *Heart of Darkness* far too much play is made with words like "inscrutable", "unfathomable", "impalpable", "mysterious", "inconceivable" in a manner that suggests an attempt to create a system or dogma of evil by sheer rhetoric. Conrad's description of the Congo is unforgettable, but his moral reflections look like stage-drawings or temporary constructions. I think the exile's temperament gave Conrad his obsession with the allusive. He could never resist a symbol; and his images tend to submerge his people at their crisis, as if they were evasions. Even so, such a concern for texture does not really explain why "Mistah Kurtz", the whole focus of *Heart of Darkness*, is a ghost or figment. His extreme lusts—what are they? What unnameable things did he do? Was he a cannibal? He murdered, we suppose. It is curious that when Marlowe actually sees the heads on the poles outside the hut, he sees them not by the defenceless naked eye but by the magnifying intervention of binoculars. At the very crisis of the story we do not directly face the fact; we are given the distortion.

Kurtz is, of course, made into an ubiquitous, diffused, romantic symbol in this manner and is the symbol of two kinds of corruption: the primordial, and the disgusting aspect of colonial exploitation in its first greedy rush. The Whites have gone mad with greed. Kurtz has simply been logical. He has gone over the borderline into "complete freedom". He has accepted the union of "desire and hate"; he has split into the prim hypocrite citizen and the savage lunatic. In love (we are led to conclude) he found "horror". All this is psychologically absorbing, for Conrad means it to apply as a potential to all of us; but it is mere hearsay in the novel. The novelist does not show us an instance of it in action.

Conrad was concerned with fear, guilt, remorse and the tincture of corruption in good things. He is preoccupied by betrayal. It is the rootless who betray. His greatness lies in the handling of a large range of moral types who suffer these evils each in a different way, so that we feel he understands a universal condition. The preoccupation stirred up certain Polish critics years ago. What crime or betrayal had Conrad on his conscience? Why did he write *Lord Jim*? What about *The Secret Agent*? His work is close to personal experience—did he commit some fault at sea? It seems certain that he did not. He may have felt, as a foreigner, the morbid anxiety that he might not come up to codes of the nation he had made his own. The Poles suggested that Conrad felt the guilt of the *emigré*, a guilt all the sharper because he was the son of a man who had been a national martyr. Conrad did not evade the criticism and answered it very sensibly. He was especially unlucky, because he reached forward prophetically to a time when exile has become, to our sense, a general experience.

List of Authors